Handbook of Human Abilities

Definitions, Measurements, and Job Task Requirements

Edwin A. Fleishman
Maureen E. Reilly

Consulting Psychologists Press, Inc.
3803 E. Bayshore Road
Palo Alto, CA 94303

For Future Editions:

Publishers, test authors, and professionals in the field of ability measurement are encouraged to submit tests or assessment materials not listed or described in this volume for consideration in future editions of this *Handbook*. Submissions should include a brief abstract, like the ones used in the *Handbook,* and an indication of the ability(s) measured by the test(s). Send to:

Handbook of Human Abilities
Attention: Edwin A. Fleishman
Department of Psychology
George Mason University
Fairfax, VA 22030-4444

Project Editor: Kathryn Buckner
Copyeditor: Dave Cole
Print Production Director: Laura Ackerman-Shaw
Manufacturing: Gloria Forbes
Cover Design: Dennis Teutschel

ISBN: 0-89106-053-7

Contents

289341

Preface

This *Handbook* brings together, for the first time, comprehensive definitions of human abilities spanning the cognitive, psychomotor, physical, and sensory/perceptual domains of human performance. A major objective of the book is to integrate these ability definitions with information about the kinds of tasks and jobs that require each ability and the tests which can be used to measure each ability. As far as we know, this is the first time this kind of integration, across the full range of human abilities, has been attempted.

We have tried to make this *Handbook* useful for personnel psychologists, human resource professionals, counselors, educational specialists, and all those who might have a need for such information. For example, we have included the addresses of test publishers as well as indexes of the jobs and tasks mentioned in the *Handbook*. The latter can assist the user in matching tests, tasks, and jobs to their ability requirements. The *Handbook* should be useful to researchers, teachers, and students concerned with individual differences in human abilities and the role of different human abilities in a variety of human performance areas. The *Handbook* provides a framework for thinking about human abilities and their measurement; consequently, we feel the Handbook can be useful in classes on individual differences, tests and measurement, personnel psychology, vocational counseling, and related areas.

This *Handbook* is a natural outgrowth of my earlier book (with Marilyn Quaintance), *Taxonomies of Human Performance: The Description of Human Tasks*. In that book, we examined alternative ways of conceptualizing and describing human tasks in order to improve predictions about human performance. That book also summarized a program of research which developed and evaluated a number of different systems for describing and classifying tasks. The objective was to develop theoretically-based language systems (taxonomies) that, when merged with appropriate sets of decision logic and appropriate sets of quantitative data, might be used to improve predictions about human performance. The assumption was that the world of human tasks is not impossibly diverse, and that common task dimensions that allow improved predictions of human performance on these tasks can be identified.

Although a number of alternative approaches for classifying tasks were evaluated, the ability requirements approach received the most extensive development and evaluation for a variety of purposes. Research with this abilities taxonomy has continued since publication of this early book, and much has been learned about the nature of these abilities, the utility of the taxonomy, the tasks and jobs which require them, and tests which measure them. We have tried to reflect this updated information in the *Handbook*.

Many of the basic concepts were originally developed in the program of research I directed sponsored by agencies of the U.S. Department of Defense. Subsequent research contributing to the system's development and application was sponsored by other government agencies, including the National Science Foundation and the National Institutes of Health, as well as many different state, county and municipal government agencies and a wide variety of industrial organizations. I am indebted to the key individuals in these agencies and companies for the support they provided.

A related development, based on this program, has been the development of a system for analyzing the ability requirements of tasks and jobs. This system involves a series of behaviorally-anchored rating scales for assessing the level of each ability required by tasks and jobs. At various times, these materials, in earlier forms and formats, have been referred to as the *Task Assessment Scales, Ability Requirement Scales,* and the *Manual for the Ability Requirement Scales* (MARS). These scales have been subsumed into the *Fleishman Job Analysis Survey* (F-JAS), which is now available through Consulting Psychologists Press. The *Handbook* allows those who use the F-JAS system to select tests of the abilities identified as required by the particular jobs of interest. There is ample research evidence that tests selected in this way turn out to have criterion-related validity. However, the *Handbook* is meant for a broader audience of professionals, practitioners, and students interested in the measurement of individual differences in abilities.

The *Administrator's Guide for the Fleishman Job Analysis Survey* (F-JAS) provides additional summaries of the research, and background and development of the ability requirements taxonomy and of its extensive application and evaluation in a wide variety of organizations. The references used in the *Handbook* will provide additional information on the construct validity of this taxonomy.

In this *Handbook*, we have used the constructs in the ability taxonomy to organize a great deal of information about human performance in the workplace. We feel it is time to use such constructs where there is a research history in establishing the network of relationships which define these constructs. We need to use a common set of definitions to provide a standardized language for use by professionals in different areas of human performance. This framework should span basic research and applied needs. There is evidence that the ability requirements taxonomy does this for a variety of purposes. This does not mean that all the constructs in this taxonomy are equally well researched, or that these constructs have captured all aspects of human performance. The taxonomy will likely be modified as future research and applications indicate.

I am indebted to many colleagues who worked with me and who contributed to the conceptual development of the ability requirements taxonomy and to its evaluation. These include, especially, George C. Theologus, Tania Romashko, George R. Wheaton, Andrew M Rose, Jerrold M. Levine, F. Mark Schemmer, Marilyn Quaintance Gowing, Michael D. Mumford, David C. Myers, Joyce C. Hogan, Deborah L. Gebhardt, Merri-Ann Cooper, and Lee Friedman. Sandra Gordon-Salant, an audiologist, and Morton Davis, an optometrist, were especially helpful with regard to measures of auditory and visual abilities. Many other individuals have contributed and many of them have been acknowledged in other publications or in their authorship of relevant research reports on these developments. I am also indebted to Kathryn Buckner, of Consulting Psychologists Press, for her technical support during the final stages of this project, to Mary Lee Peterson for her administrative and clerical support, and, as usual, to my wife, Pauline, for her continued encouragement and support. I am especially grateful to Maureen E. Reilly for her scholarship and persistence in coauthoring this *Handbook* with me.

Edwin A. Fleishman
George Mason University
Fairfax, Virginia

Introduction

This *Handbook* is a guide to tests which measure cognitive, psychomotor, physical, and sensory/perceptual abilities, as defined by Fleishman's ability requirements approach for classifying tasks (Fleishman, 1975, 1982; Fleishman & Quaintance, 1984). As the use of the *Fleishman Job Analysis Survey* (F-JAS), formerly known as the *Manual for the Ability Requirements Scales* (MARS), has continued, practitioners have expressed a need for a guide which provides information about the tests which measure each ability. The *Handbook of Human Abilities* has been designed to meet that need. In addition to information about the tests, the *Handbook* provides examples of tasks which are representative of each ability, and identifies jobs requiring each ability. The *Handbook* also provides precise definitions of each ability based on current research. This is the first publication that brings all this information together. The *Handbook* is a useful tool, independent of the F-JAS materials.

Objectives of the Handbook

The *Handbook* provides guidance for personnel psychologists, counselors, and educational and human resource specialists in selecting tests that may match the requirements of jobs developed through job and occupational analysis procedures. When the F-JAS is used as the job analysis tool, the *Handbook* provides test options linked directly to the ability requirements identified. Its objective is to provide a useful, integrative summary of abilities, tasks, jobs, and tests. However, the *Handbook* is also a more general reference source. In this capacity, it provides a framework for thinking about the domain of human abilities by bringing together information from several ability domains often treated separately (i.e., cognitive, psychomotor, physical, and sensory/perceptual).

1

Format of the Handbook

The *Handbook* has four sections. Section I provides basic information on each of 52 abilities. For each ability, the reader is provided with a definition based on current research regarding the nature of that ability. This is followed by examples of tasks requiring that ability. The tasks described were selected to be both representative and diverse enough to show the range of activities encompassed by that ability. Next, examples are provided of jobs or occupations that require this ability. Finally, a sampling of specific tests to measure that ability are described.

Section II provides a more comprehensive listing of tests, authors, and publishers classified by each ability.

Section III provides complete addresses of all test publishers referred to in the *Handbook*.

Section IV provides the citations for literature mentioned or cited in the text.

Section V provides indexes of tasks and jobs mentioned in this *Handbook*. This provides a quick reference to match tasks and jobs with their ability requirements and the tests that measure these abilities.

Development of the Handbook

Fleishman's ability requirements taxonomy was developed to provide the widest variety of task-performance descriptions using the fewest independent ability categories. This was accomplished via a careful review of the factor-analytic research on human abilities, including the author's extensive research on the organization of human abilities. The resulting list of abilities draws from the cognitive, perceptual, psychomotor, and physical domains. Later, sensory/perceptual abilities, including vision and audition, were added to the taxonomy, resulting in a list of 52 abilities.

The ability requirements approach assumes that, although some abilities are more malleable than others, an ability is a relatively enduring general trait or capacity that is related to performance across a variety of tasks. This assumes that tasks differ in the extent to which an ability is required for successful performance. Furthermore, individuals differ in their status on different abilities. Thus, Fleishman's ability requirements taxonomy allows for a match of the individual's ability profile with the ability requirements of the job.

This *Handbook* is a logical extension of the book, *Taxonomies of Human Performance* (Fleishman & Quaintance, 1984), and the continuing research program of Fleishman and associates on identifying the ability requirements of human tasks (summarized in Fleishman, 1975, 1982; Fleishman & Mumford, 1988).

A variety of sources were consulted in order to identify relevant tests for the 52 abilities in the taxonomy. These sources include assessment reference guides (Conoley & Kramer, 1989; Katz, 1985; Mitchell, 1983; Psychological Tests and Special Education Materials, 1989; Sweetland & Keyser, 1986), test manuals (Ekstrom, French, & Harman, 1979; Stubblefield, 1987), test catalogs (Lafayette Instrument Co., Inc.; Stoelting Co.), textbooks (Aiken, 1988; Anastasi, 1988; Cronbach, 1990; Fleishman, 1964, 1972; Guilford & Hoepfner, 1971; Harman, 1975; Linn, 1989; Sternberg & Smith, 1988; Yost & Nielsen, 1985), journal articles, and technical reports (Schemmer, 1982; Stephens & Prasansuk, 1988; Weldon, Yarkin-Levin & Fleishman, 1982). Where possible, an attempt was made to include examples of tests and tasks appropriate for education, business, industrial, government, and military settings.

Another earlier compendium was the Educational Testing Service Kit of Reference Tests, a set of tests recommended by experts and based on factor analysis research (Ekstrom, French, Harman & Dermen, 1976). The Educational Testing Service kit suggests tests for research, but does not include jobs and task linkages or tests in the psychomotor, physical, and sensory/perceptual domains.

While the selection of tests to assess the abilities was based primarily on previous research, often professional judgment was necessary. For example, optometrists and audiologists were consulted on visual and auditory and sensory/perceptual measures. The *Handbook* is not intended to be comprehensive; it provides only a sampling of tests for each ability. Tests used for special purposes, such as neuropsychological evaluation, or tests used exclusively for special groups, such as blind or deaf individuals, were not included.

The selection of tests was restricted to those appropriate for measuring adult abilities, and group tests were preferred over tests requiring individual administration. Additionally, where possible, the abilities have been linked to tests from some of the better-known test batteries (e.g., *Employee Aptitude Survey, Flanagan Aptitude Battery, General Aptitude Test Battery, Guilford-Zimmerman Aptitude Survey, Occupational Aptitude Survey*). For evaluative reviews of many of these tests listed in the *Handbook,* the reader may want to consult Buros' *Mental Measurement Yearbook* (Conoley & Kramer, 1989).

Readers who wish more background on the development of the human abilities taxonomy can consult Fleishman and Quaintance (1984) and chapters and articles on the research background of the ability concepts (Fleishman, 1964, 1972, 1975, 1982, 1988; Fleishman & Mumford, 1988, 1989, 1991). The latest edition of the *Fleishman Job Analysis Survey* (Fleishman, 1992; Fleishman & Reilly, 1992) provides the job analysis tool for assessing the ability requirements of specific jobs.

Section I

Ability Definitions,
Tasks, Jobs,
and Test Descriptions

1. Oral Comprehension

Definition: Oral comprehension is the ability to understand spoken English words and sentences. This ability involves listening to and understanding the meaning of words, phrases, sentences, and paragraphs. It involves receiving spoken information and understanding it. It does not involve receiving and understanding written information or giving oral information.

Tasks: Oral comprehension may be used in listening to and understanding lectures or instructions, descriptions of events, places, or people, and telephone, television, or radio messages.

Jobs: Jobs that require high levels of oral comprehension include those of a manager, judge, reporter, executive, professor, interpreter, and psychiatrist.

Test Examples: Tests of oral comprehension usually require subjects to listen to a tape-recorded passage of information and then answer written questions about the content of the recording.

The PSI Basic Skills Tests for Business, Industry, & Government: Following Oral Directions—BST #7
Psychological Services, Inc.

Subjects listen to a 6.5 minute tape recording about clerical and office duties. The tape is played only once and they are encouraged to take written notes. They then complete a 24-item multiple-choice test about the content of the tape. The test takes five minutes to administer.

Watson-Barker Listening Test
SPECTRA Communications Associates

This test requires subjects to listen to audiotaped material and answer questions on the following areas: Evaluating Message Content, Understanding Meaning in Conversations, Understanding and Remembering Information in Lectures, Evaluating Emotional Meanings in Messages, Following Instructions and Directions, and Total (comprehension). The test has two forms with 50 items on each form. It takes 30 minutes to complete each form. Normative data are available for college students and adults in business and professional jobs.

Cognitive Abilities

2. Written Comprehension

Definition: Written comprehension is the ability to understand written sentences and paragraphs. This ability involves reading and understanding the meaning of words, phrases, sentences, and paragraphs. It involves reading; it does not involve writing, listening to, or understanding spoken information.

Tasks: Written comprehension may be used in reading books, articles, technical manuals, written instructions, work orders, and apartment leases.

Jobs: Jobs that require high levels of written comprehension include those of an administrator, lawyer, reporter, scientist, translator, and journal editor.

Test Examples: Tests of written comprehension usually present subjects with one or more passages of information. They then answer multiple-choice questions about the information. The emphasis of the test may be on following directions, understanding the general meaning of paragraphs, or understanding the meaning of specific words. Other tests of written comprehension are strictly vocabulary-oriented, focusing on identifying definitions, synonyms, or antonyms.

Guilford-Zimmerman Aptitude Survey: Verbal Comprehension
Consulting Psychologists Press

This test measures the ability to understand the meaning of words using a 72-item multiple-choice test. Twenty-five minutes are allowed to complete the test. It has been used to assess academic aptitude and suitability for fields in which reading ability is an important factor. Normative data are provided for college groups.

Advanced Vocabulary Test II—V-5
Educational Testing Service
reprinted by permission of Educational Testing Service, the copyright owner

This is a four-choice synonym test consisting mainly of difficult items. It measures verbal facility and was adapted from a test by J.B. Carroll (Carroll, 1980). Subjects are given a word and are asked to choose which of four alternatives has the same, or nearly the same, meaning. This test has two parts, each with 18 items. Four minutes are allowed to complete each part. It is suitable for research and experimental use with students in grades 11 through 16.

Understanding Communication
London House Press

This test measures comprehension of verbal material in short sentences and phrases. It consists of 40 items and takes 15 minutes to complete. Basic reading skills are required. It has been used for industrial screening and selection of skilled occupational groups that need to understand written material and communications.

The PSI Basic Skills Tests for Business, Industry, and Government: Reading Comprehension—BST #2
Psychological Services, Inc.

Subjects listen to a 6.5 minute tape recording about clerical and office duties. The tape is played only once and they are encouraged to take written notes. They then complete a 24-item multiple-choice test about the content of the tape. The test takes five minutes to administer. It has been used to select clerical and office workers.

Nelson-Denny Reading Test: Forms E & F
The Riverside Publishing Co.

This test has two parts: a vocabulary test that measures vocabulary development, and a comprehension test that assesses comprehension and reading rate. The test has 136 paper-pencil items and provides a standard score scale. 35 minutes are allowed to complete it. It is suitable for adolescents and adults, and has been used to assess student achievement and progress in vocabulary, comprehension, and reading rate. Forms G and H, available in the Spring of 1992, have 118 items.

Cognitive Abilities

3. Oral Expression

Definition: Oral expression is the ability to use English words or sentences in speaking so others can understand. It includes the ability to orally communicate information and the meaning of ideas to other people. This ability involves knowledge of the distinctions between words, and of how words should be put together to communicate the intended meaning of a message.

This ability does not involve writing words or sentences, nor does it involve understanding spoken or written words or sentences. It deals with how well someone can explain orally spoken ideas, rather than with the number of ideas or the creativity of the ideas.

Tasks: Oral expression is involved in giving instructions or directions, presenting a speech, and in describing an event.

Jobs: Jobs that require high levels of oral expression include those of a politician, manager, lawyer, actor, recruiter, senator, college professor, preacher, and sales agent.

Test Examples: Oral expression is usually assessed in an interview or in an assessment center. No standard tests of oral expression were identified.

Cognitive Abilities

---

4. Written Expression

Definition: Written expression is the ability to use English words or sentences in writing so others can understand. It includes the ability to communicate information and ideas in writing. This ability involves knowledge of grammar, the meaning of words, distinctions between words, and how to organize sentences and paragraphs.

This ability does not involve speaking words or sentences, nor does it involve understanding spoken or written words or sentences. It deals with how well one can explain ideas in written form, rather than with the number of ideas or their creativity.

Tasks: Written expression is involved in writing articles, technical manuals, instructions, job recommendations, letters, and memos.

Jobs: Jobs that require high levels of written expression include those of an administrator, judge, reporter, research scientist, author, and speech writer.

Test Examples: Tests of written expression usually present subjects with written material. They are then asked to formulate a written response to the presented stimulus.

The Ennis-Weir Critical Thinking Essay Test
Critical Thinking Press and Software, formerly Midwest Publications

This test measures an individual's ability to critically evaluate an argument and formulate a written responding argument. Subjects are given a letter to the editor of a newspaper in a fictitious city regarding parking problems. They are instructed to respond in writing to each argument presented in the letter, evaluate the overall quality of the argument of the stimulus letter, and defend their evaluation. The test takes 40 minutes to complete.

Cognitive Abilities

---

5. Fluency of Ideas

Definition: Fluency of ideas is the ability to produce a number of ideas about a given topic. This ability concerns the number of ideas generated rather than the quality, correctness, or creativity of the ideas. It deals with generating a number of ideas, rather than conveying these ideas clearly to others. It differs from category flexibility in that it focuses purely on the number of ideas rather than on the number of categories from which the ideas are generated.

Tasks: Fluency of ideas may be used in thinking of a number of alternative solutions to a problem, different uses of a new tool, alternative possibilities for examining and fixing equipment malfunctions, and generating alternative names for a product.

Jobs: Jobs that require a high level of fluency of ideas include those of an inventor, advertising executive, product designer, song writer, and interior designer.

Test Examples: Tests of fluency of ideas are usually open-ended. They require subjects to generate as many words or ideas as possible about a given theme or topic within a specified time frame.

Alternate Uses
Consulting Psychologists Press

This is a multiple-item paper-pencil test that requires subjects to produce a variety of ideas relating to the use of an object. Normative data are available for sixth-grade, ninth-grade, and college students. Eight minutes are allowed to complete the test. It has been used for research and experimental purposes.

Consequences
Consulting Psychologists Press

Subjects are required to write consequences for five new and unusual situations. The test takes ten minutes to complete. Normative data are available. It has been used for research and experimental purposes.

Ideational Fluency
Consulting Psychologists Press

Subjects are required to efficiently produce many ideas fulfilling meaningful specifications. The test is open-ended, has multiple items, and takes 12 minutes to complete. It has been used in research and experimental applications.

Topics Test—F-1

Educational Testing Service

reprinted by permission of Educational Testing Service, the copyright owner

This test, which measures ideational fluency, requires subjects to write as many ideas as possible about a given topic. It has two parts, with 4 minutes allowed for each part. It is suitable for research use with students in grades 8 through 16.

Cognitive Abilities

6. Originality

Definition: Originality is the ability to produce unusual or clever ideas about a given topic or situation. It is the ability to invent creative solutions to problems or to develop new procedures for situations in which standard operating procedures do not apply.

This ability emphasizes the creativity and quality of an idea rather than the number of ideas produced or how well these ideas are communicated to others. It involves generating creative solutions rather than discovering logical solutions or recognizing the problem in the first place. Originality refers to divergent thinking; that is, it does not involve following a logical path to a solution.

Tasks: Originality can be applied to the invention of a new tool to deal with an equipment repair problem, or the development of a new idea for personnel recruitment or job enrichment, discovery of a novel use for a product, and developing a new musical form or new style of painting.

Jobs: Jobs that require high levels of originality include those of an architect, playwright, poet, cartoonist, artist, musical composer, and choreographer.

Test Examples: Tests of originality are usually open-ended and require subjects to spontaneously produce creative ideas about a related topic.

Consequences
Consulting Psychologists Press

Subjects are required to write consequences for five new and unusual situations. The test takes ten minutes to complete. Normative data are available. It has been used for research and experimental purposes.

Cognitive Abilities

7. Memorization

Definition: Memorization is the ability to remember information, such as words, numbers, pictures, and procedures. Pieces of information can be remembered by themselves or with other pieces of information. This ability emphasizes what cognitive psychologists call *episodic memory,* which is the memory for specific events. This can be distinguished from *semantic memory,* which refers to the memory of general knowledge.

Tasks: Examples of episodic memory include memory for new names, faces, codes, telephone numbers, geographic locations, documents, long lists, and bus numbers.

Jobs: Jobs that require high levels of memorization include those of an actor, lawyer, insurance sales agent, tax accountant, medical doctor, and concert pianist.

Test Examples: Tests of memorization require subjects to recall or recognize verbal, visual, or numerical information. Subjects may, for instance, be presented with information in categories and then be asked to recognize or reproduce the correct categories.

Benton Revised Visual Retention Test
The Psychological Corporation

Subjects view designs one at a time and then attempt to reproduce each design exactly by drawing it on plain paper. Five minutes are allowed to complete this test, which must be individually administered. It has been used for mental examinations and in experimental research.

The PSI Basic Skills Tests for Business, Industry, and Government: Memory BST #16
Psychological Services, Inc.

Subjects are given five minutes to study a reference list presenting the names of five building supply companies in each of five categories (plumbing, heating, lighting, roofing, and flooring). They then have five minutes to recall the information presented on the list. This test has been used to select clerical and office workers.

Cognitive Abilities

8. Problem Sensitivity

Definition: Problem sensitivity is the ability to know when something is wrong or is likely to go wrong. It includes being able to identify the whole problem as well as the elements of a problem. It does not involve the ability to solve a problem, only the ability to recognize that there is a problem.

Tasks: Problem sensitivity is involved in recognizing symptoms of equipment malfunction, the early stage of an illness, the likelihood of a prison riot, and the accuracy of data received.

Jobs: Jobs that require high levels of problem sensitivity include those of a computer programmer, medical doctor, plant manager, air traffic controller, fire inspector, and aircraft technician.

Test Examples: Tests of problem sensitivity present subjects with a plan or scenario and ask them to list the faults or problems that may arise. No standard tests of problem sensitivity were identified.

Cognitive Abilities

---

9. Mathematical Reasoning

Definition: Mathematical reasoning is the ability to understand and organize a problem and then to select a mathematical method or formula to solve the problem. It encompasses reasoning through mathematical problems to determine appropriate operations that can be performed to solve problems. It also includes the understanding or structuring of mathematical problems. The actual manipulation of numbers is not included in this ability.

Tasks: Mathematical reasoning is involved in developing the mathematical equations for describing the course of a missile launch, applying a method for analyzing production data, determining the area of a building, and deciding how to calculate business profits.

Jobs: Jobs that require high levels of mathematical reasoning include those of an engineer, mathematician, statistician, and physicist.

Test Examples: Tests of mathematical reasoning are sometimes referred to as tests of general reasoning or problem solving. These tests usually present subjects with a short word problem that requires a numerical answer. Calculations are sometimes required; however, the emphasis is always on understanding the problem and applying the appropriate solution.

Guilford-Zimmerman Aptitude Survey: General Reasoning
Consulting Psychologists Press

This is a multiple-choice, paper-pencil test consisting of arithmetic-reasoning items graded in difficulty. Numerical computation is kept to a minimum, removing most of the numerical-facility component from the measure. The results yield C-scale, centile, and T-scale norms for college groups. Thirty-five minutes are allowed to complete the test and it is suitable for group use. It has been used as an aptitude test for a variety of problem-solving tasks.

The PSI Basic Skills tests for Business, Industry, and Government: Problem Solving (BST #5)
Psychological Services, Inc.

This is a 24-item, paper-pencil, multiple-choice test. It consists of short word problems that require a numerical answer. The test emphasizes determining the arithmetic problem contained in the story, rather than lengthy computations. Ten minutes are allowed to complete the test. It has been used to select clerical and office workers.

Technical Test Battery: Numerical Reasoning (TTB:NT6)
Saville & Holdsworth Ltd.

This is a 30-item, paper-pencil, multiple-choice test consisting of short numerical problems set in a technical context. Some calculation is involved, but the emphasis is on understanding, reasoning, and recognizing shortcut methods. The problems cover the basic arithmetic operations, percentages, fractions, decimals, angles, graphs, simple technical drawings, metric lengths, areas, and volumes. The questions all have a technical slant, dealing with materials, output, production methods, etc. Ten minutes are allowed to complete the test. It has been used in the selection and development of technical staff, including apprentices.

Cognitive Abilities

10. Number Facility

Definition: Number facility is the ability to add, subtract, multiply, divide, and manipulate numbers quickly and accurately. It is required for steps in other operations, such as finding percentages and taking square roots. This ability does not involve understanding or organizing mathematical problems.

Tasks: Number facility is involved in filling out income tax returns, keeping track of financial accounts, computing interest payments, adding up a restaurant bill, and balancing a checkbook.

Jobs: Jobs that require high levels of number facility include those of an accountant, audit clerk, bookkeeper, cashier, and teller.

Test Examples: Tests of number facility usually require subjects to quickly perform numerical operations such as addition or subtraction. Tests of this type require subjects to either provide the correct answer or choose the correct answer from multiple-choice items.

Guilford-Zimmerman Aptitude Survey: Numerical Operations
Consulting Psychologists Press

This is a paper-pencil, multiple-choice test including simple problems of addition, subtraction, and multiplication. The results yield C-scale, centile, and T-scale norms for college groups. Eight minutes are allowed to complete the test. It has been used with accountants, sales persons, and many types of clerical workers.

Addition Test—N-1
Educational Testing Service
reprinted by permission of Educational Testing Service, the copyright owner

On this test of number facility, subjects are asked to quickly and accurately add sets of three 1- or 2-digit numbers. They are told that the test is speeded, so they should not expect to finish all of the problems in the time allowed. The test has 2 parts and allows 2 minutes for each part. It has been used for research and experimental purposes with students in grades 6 to 16.

Employee Aptitude Survey Test #2—Numerical Ability (EAS #2)
Psychological Services, Inc.

This 75-item, paper–pencil, multiple-choice test assesses addition, subtraction, multiplication, and division skills. Ten minutes are allowed to complete the test. It has been used to select and place executives, supervisors, engineers, accountants, sales, and clerical workers.

Shop Arithmetic Test
Richardson, Bellows, Henry & Co., Inc.

This is a 20-item, paper–pencil test of mathematical abilities related to industrial situations. It includes simple arithmetic operations (fractions and decimal fractions form the upper limit) involved in figuring sums or remainders on problems of weight or length; computing measures of distance, area, or volume; and analyzing operations data from tables. The test is available in two forms. Form I was normed on male managers and executives, technical and engineering supervisors, industrial foremen and supervisors, and mechanical and operating employees and applicants. Form II, which is slightly easier than Form I, was normed on male industrial applicants and mechanical and operating employees. Fifteen minutes are allowed to complete the test. It has been used with applicants for operations and craft positions and engineering aides.

Cognitive Abilities

---

11. Deductive Reasoning

Definition: Deductive reasoning is the ability to apply general rules to specific problems and to come up with logical answers; for example, deciding whether or not an answer to a non–mathematical problem makes sense, or solving syllogistic reasoning problems. This ability involves applying general rules to specific problems rather than forming general rules from separate pieces of information.

Tasks: Deductive reasoning is involved in deciding which route to take when considering time, cost, and geography; designing a new aircraft wing using aerodynamics principles; deciding what factors to consider in selecting stocks, and deciding if particular laws have been violated by certain actions in criminal cases.

Jobs: Jobs that require high levels of deductive reasoning include those of an engineer, mathematician, operations–research analyst, computer programmer, physicist, judge, auto mechanic, and pathologist.

Test Examples: Tests of deductive reasoning usually present subjects with a set of facts. Given a set of multiple-choice items, subjects are required to select the conclusion that follows from the facts.

Nonsense Syllogisms Test—RL-1
Educational Testing Service
reprinted by permission of Educational Testing Service, the copyright owner

In this test of logical reasoning, subjects are presented with formal syllogisms using nonsensical content which cannot be solved by reference to past learning. Some of the stated conclusions follow correctly from the premises and some do not. The task is to indicate whether or not the conclusion is logically correct. The test has two parts, with 15 items each, and 4 minutes are allowed for each part. It is suitable for grades 11 through 16 and is used in research and experimental applications.

*The PSI Basic Skills Tests for Business, Industry, and Government:
Reasoning (BST #10)*
Psychological Services, Inc.

Subjects are required to draw valid, logical conclusions from factual
information. They are presented with lists of facts and told to choose,
from multiple-choice items, the conclusion that follows from each
list. The test takes five minutes to complete. It has been used to select
clerical and office workers.

Employee Aptitude Survey Test #7—Verbal Reasoning (EAS #7)
Psychological Services, Inc.

This is a 30-item, paper-pencil, multiple-choice test consisting of six
lists of facts (one-sentence statements), each with five possible conclusions. Subjects read each list of facts and then look at each conclusion
and decide whether it is definitely true, definitely false, or unknown
from the given facts. Five minutes are allowed to complete the test. It
has been used to select employees for jobs requiring the ability to
organize, evaluate, and use information (including administrative and
technical decision making, supervisory, scientific, and accounting
abilities). It has also been used in career counseling.

Advanced Test Battery: Verbal Critical Reasoning (ATB-VA3)
Saville & Holdsworth Ltd.

This is a 60-item, paper-pencil, multiple-choice, test consisting of
complex passages and a number of statements that might be made in
connection with each. The statements must be evaluated in terms of
whether they, their opposite, or neither, logically follow from the
passage in question. The passages sample a wide range of material
from social policy to medicine, all of which could be on the agenda
of a management meeting. The test has a high degree of apparent
relevance to the assessment of managerial reasoning skills. Thirty
minutes are allowed to complete the test. It has been used for management selection and graduate recruitment.

Cognitive Abilities

---

12. Inductive Reasoning

Definition: Inductive reasoning is the ability to combine separate pieces of information, or specific answers to non–mathematical problems, or to form general rules or conclusions. It involves the ability to think of possible reasons why things go together, such as giving a logical explanation for a series of events that seem unrelated. It involves forming the best general rule, rather than producing many rules or applying a previously formed rule. It is sometimes seen as the forming and testing of hypotheses.

Tasks: Inductive reasoning is involved in diagnosing a disease using knowledge from many lab test results; forecasting the weather from information on wind current, barometric pressure, and other information; determining the guilty parties from available evidence, and predicting election results based on demographics, polls and voting trends.

Jobs: Jobs that require high levels of inductive reasoning include those of a statistician, psychologist, medical doctor, juror, and meteorologist.

Test Examples: Tests of inductive reasoning usually require subjects to discover rules in patterns of figures or written information, or to make interpretations of data.

Letter Sets—I-1
Educational Testing Service
reprinted by permission of Educational Testing Service, the copyright owner

In this test of inductive reasoning, subjects are presented with five sets of four letters. The task is to find the rule that relates four of the sets to each other and mark the set that does not fit the rule. Each of the two parts has 15 items and seven minutes are allowed for each part. This test is suitable for grades 8 through16 and has been used in research and experimental applications.

Locations Test— I-2
Educational Testing Service
reprinted by permission of Educational Testing Service, the copyright owner

In this test of inductive reasoning, each item has five rows of dashes and gaps. In each of the first four rows one place is marked according to a rule. The task is to discover the rule and to mark the fifth row accordingly. The test has two parts. Each part has 14 items and six minutes are allowed for each part. This test has been used in research and experimental applications with students in grades 8 through 16.

Advanced Test Battery: Numerical Critical Reasoning (ATB:NA4)
Saville & Holdsworth, Ltd.

This is a high level 40-item, multiple-choice paper and pencil test. Applicants are required to make inferences from numerical or statistical data. The test has been used in selection for general managers and jobs involving development of senior managerial staff, and graduate recruitment. The test takes 35 minutes to complete.

Critical Reasoning Test Battery (CRTB)
Saville & Holdsworth Ltd.

This battery consists of three paper-pencil, multiple-choice tests. The Verbal Evaluation Test is a 60-item test measuring the ability to understand and evaluate the logic of various types of arguments. The Interpreting Data Test is a 40-item test measuring the ability to make correct decisions or inferences from numerical or statistical data that is presented as tables or diagrams. The Diagrammatic Series Test is a 40-item test measuring the ability to reason with diagrams, and requires the candidate to discover logical rules governing sequences of symbols and diagrams. Each test takes 20–30 minutes to complete. The tests have been used in the selection and development of educationally qualified school-leavers and junior and middle management. It has also been used for guidance and placement of students planning to attend a university.

Cognitive Abilities

13. Information Ordering

Definition: Information ordering is the ability to correctly follow a rule or set of rules specifying how to arrange things or actions in a certain order. The rule or set of rules used must be given. The things or actions to be put in order can include numbers, letters, words, pictures, procedures, sentences, and mathematical or logical operations. This ability involves following a previously given rule rather than producing rules or using rules to solve problems.

Tasks: Information ordering is involved in applying first aid in a life-threatening situation, following a check-out procedure in operating equipment, arranging sentences into a meaningful paragraph, and putting items in numerical or alphabetical order.

Jobs: Jobs that require high levels of information ordering include those of an archivist, accountant, pilot, file clerk, librarian, and astronaut.

Test Examples: Tests of information ordering present subjects with a list of words, sentences, events, or objects. Subjects are asked to order the list according to a given specification.

Ordering I
Cited in Guilford & Hoepfner, 1971

Subjects are given short lists of events and told to put them into the most reasonable chronological order.

Cognitive Abilities

14. Category Flexibility

Definition: Category flexibility is the ability to produce many rules in such a way that each rule tells how to group a set of things in a different way. Each different group must contain at least two things from the original set. This ability involves producing many rules rather than producing one best rule, or applying previously given rules.

Tasks: Category flexibility is involved in classifying synthetic fibers in terms of their strength, cost, elasticity, and melting points; classifying flowers according to size, color, odor, and use; and sorting nails in a tool box on the basis of length.

Jobs: Jobs that require high levels of category flexibility include those of an archivist, museum curator, librarian, and biology taxonomist.

Test Examples: Tests of category flexibility usually present a list of items. Subjects are required to form meaningful categories with the items. They may also be required to provide a reason for the category formation.

Combining Objects—XU-1
Educational Testing Services
reprinted by permission of Educational Testing Service, the copyright owner

In this test of flexibility of use, subjects are instructed to name two objects that can be used together in order to make or do something. Subjects are presented with a request, and given the location where this is taking place. The test has two parts with 10 items each. Five minutes are allowed to complete each part. This test has been used in research and experimental applications with students in grades 9 through 16.

Different Uses—XU-4
Educational Testing Service
reprinted by permission of Educational Testing Service, the copyright owner

In this test of flexibility of use, subjects are asked to think of up to six different uses for common objects. They are presented with an object followed by its common use, and are asked to write down other ways in which the object could be used. Scores are based on the number of changes of use, not on the total number of responses. The test has two parts with 4 items each, and 5 minutes are allowed to complete each part. It is suitable for grades 6 through 16 and has been used in research and experimental applications.

Halstead Category Test
Precision People, Inc.

This computer-administered, multiple-item test is used to assess individuals' ability to categorize graphic items along a number of different dimensions. Subjects are presented with a series of graphic items on the screen. They are told to choose whether an object belongs to or differs from a set of objects. The series gradually increases in difficulty. This is an untimed, computer-scored test.

Cognitive Abilities

---

15. Speed of Closure

Definition: Speed of closure is the ability to quickly make sense of information which initially seems to be without meaning or organization. It involves the degree to which different pieces of information can be quickly combined and organized into one meaningful pattern. All the pieces of information presented are relevant to the task, but the meaningful pattern is not known beforehand. The material may be either visual or auditory. This contrasts with flexibility of closure, in which the pattern or object one is looking for is known but embedded in distracting background information.

Tasks: Speed of closure may be used in interpreting weather radar scope patterns to decide if the weather is changing, receiving Morse code, making sense out of strange handwriting, reading a coded message and figuring out the code, and recognizing a melody from just a few notes.

Jobs: Jobs that require high levels of speed of closure include those of a meteorologist, cryptographer, navigator, and radio telegrapher.

Test Examples: Tests of speed of closure usually present pictures or words that are partially obscured, incomplete, or similarly ambiguous. Subjects are required to identify the picture or word. These tests are usually open-ended.

Concealed Words—CS-2
Educational Testing Service
reprinted by permission of Educational Testing Service, the copyright owner

This test of speed of closure presents words which have parts of each letter missing. Subjects are required to write out the full word in an adjacent space. Each of the test's two parts has 25 words and 4 minutes are allowed for each part. The test is suitable for grades 6 through 16 and has been used in research and experimental applications.

Gestalt Completion Test—CS-1
Educational Testing Service
reprinted by permission of Educational Testing Service, the copyright owner

In this test of speed of closure (the ability to unite an apparently disparate perceptual field), subjects are presented with incomplete pictures and asked to write down what they think the picture is, being as specific as possible. This test has two parts, with 10 pictures per part. Two minutes are allowed per part. The test has been used in research and experimental applications with students in grades 6 through 16.

Closure Speed (Gestalt Completion)
London House Press

This is a 24-item, paper-pencil test measuring the subject's ability to construct a total picture from incomplete or ambiguous material. Three minutes are allowed to complete the test. It has been used for evaluation of perceptual skills.

Cognitive Abilities

16. Flexibility of Closure

Definition: Flexibility of closure is the ability to identify or detect a known pattern (e.g., a figure, word, or object) that is hidden in other material. The task is to pick out the disguised pattern from the background material. Recognizing the distracting background material is part of the task to be accomplished.

Tasks: Flexibility of closure is involved in picking out a target that is camouflaged, finding the switches in a complicated wiring diagram or floor plan, looking for a golf ball in the rough, and picking out a camouflaged vehicle in a forest.

Jobs: Jobs that require high levels of flexibility of closure include those of a microbiologist, radar operator, radiologist, electronics maintenance personnel, and pilot.

Test Examples: Tests of flexibility of closure usually present a set of approximately five simple figures and one complex pattern. Subjects must indicate which of the simple figures is imbedded in the more complex pattern. Conversely, one simple figure may be presented, followed by a series of complex patterns. In this case, subjects are required to indicate which of the complex patterns contains the simple figure. Some tests allow for more than one correct answer.

Hidden Figures Test—CF-1 (rev.)
Educational Testing Service
reprinted by permission of Educational Testing Service, the copyright owner

In this test of flexibility of closure, subjects are required to decide which of five geometrical figures is embedded in a complex pattern. This test has two parts with 16 items per part. Twelve minutes are allowed per part. It has been used in research and experimental applications with students in grades 8 through 16.

Closure Flexibility (Concealed Figures)
London House Press

This 49-item, paper-pencil test requires subjects to detect a given figure embedded in a larger, more complex drawing. For example, after being presented with a figure, subjects indicate in which of four drawings that figure appears. Ten minutes are allowed to complete the test. It has been used by vocational counselors to predict mechanical skills and possible success in the engineering and drafting professions.

Cognitive Abilities

17. Spatial Orientation

Definition: Spatial orientation is the ability to know one's location in relation to the environment one is in or to know where an object is in relation to oneself. It involves maintaining directional orientation in one's bearings with respect to the points on a compass. This ability allows one to stay oriented in a vehicle as it changes location and direction. It helps prevent disorientation while in a new environment.

Tasks: Spatial orientation is involved in aircraft piloting, negotiating in a gravity-free environment, using a road map in a city, moving through a dark room, and using a floor plan to locate oneself in a shopping mall.

Jobs: Jobs that require high levels of spatial orientation include those of a cartographer, taxi driver, surveyor, pilot, navigator, and astronaut.

Test Examples: Tests of spatial orientation usually present subjects with a figure or scene. Subjects are asked to indicate (by selecting from a set of alternatives), how the scene would look from a different (specified) direction or they are shown the scene and asked the position of the observer. Sometimes use of a compass is included in the task.

Guilford-Zimmerman Aptitude Survey: Spatial Orientation
Consulting Psychologists Press

This test measures the ability to perceive spatial arrangements. It is relevant to the operation of machines for which there is a choice of direction of movement in response to visual displays. Multiple-choice items measure the cognition of figural systems. Ten minutes are allowed to complete the test.

Project A (U.S. Army): Orientation Test 1
Cited in Olson, 1990

Direction Orientation Form B, developed by researchers in the Army Air Force (AAF) Aviation Psychology Program, serves as a marker for this test. Subjects are presented with six circles. In the test's original form, the first circle indicates the compass direction for North. For most items, North is rotated out of its conventional position. Compass directions also appear on the remaining five circles. Subjects must determine for each circle whether or not the direction indicated was correctly positioned by comparing it to the direction of North in the first circle.

Project A (U.S. Army): Orientation Test 3
Cited in Olson, 1990

This test was modeled after another spatial orientation test, Compass
Directions, developed in the AAF Aviation Psychology Program.
Orientation Test 3 presents subjects with a map that includes various
landmarks (e.g., a barracks, a campsite, a forest, a lake). Within each
item, subjects are provided with compass directions that indicate the
direction from one landmark to another, (e.g., "the forest is North of
the campsite"). Subjects are also informed of their present location
relative to another landmark. Given this information, subjects must
determine which direction to go to reach yet another structure or
landmark. Different compass directions are given for each item.

Cognitive Abilities

18. Visualization

Definition: Visualization is the ability to imagine how something will look when it is moved around or when its parts are moved or rearranged. This ability requires the forming of mental images of how patterns or objects would look after certain changes, such as unfolding or rotation. One has to predict how an object, set of objects, or pattern will appear after the changes have been made.

Tasks: Visualization is involved in anticipating one's opponent's as well as one's own future moves in a game of chess or checkers, knowing how to cut and fold a piece of paper to make a cube, anticipating how furniture will look in a room when it is rearranged or how boxes should be placed on a shelf so they will fit, reading blueprints, and imagining how to put paper in the typewriter so the letter head comes out at the top.

Jobs: Jobs that require high levels of visualization include those of an architect, engineer, drafter, mechanic, and dentist.

Test Examples: Tests of visualization usually present subjects with a figure or pieces of a disassembled figure. Subjects are required to indicate from multiple-choice items how the figure would look when rearranged or assembled.

Form Board Test—VZ-1
Educational Testing Service
reprinted by permission of Educational Testing Service, the copyright owner

In this test of visualization ability, subjects are presented with 5 shaded drawings of pieces, some of which can be put together to form a figure which is presented in outline form. The task is to indicate which of the pieces, when fitted together, would fit the outline. Each part has 24 items and 8 minutes are allowed for each part. The test is suitable for grades 9 through 16 and has been used in research and experimental applications.

Paper Folding—VZ-2
Educational Testing Service
reprinted by permission of Educational Testing Service, the copyright owner

For each item on this test of visualization, successive drawings illustrate two or three folds being made in a square sheet of paper. The final drawing of the folded paper shows where a hole has been punched. Subjects select one of the 5 drawings to show how the punched sheet would appear when fully reopened. Each part has 10 items and 3 minutes are allowed for each part. The test is suitable for grades 9 through 16 and has been used in research and experimental applications.

Technical Test Battery: Spatial Recognition (TTB:ST9)
Saville & Holdsworth Ltd.

This test, consisting of 40 items, is used to select engineering apprentices or technical operators. It requires applicants to recognize shapes in two dimensions after they have been rotated. A series of shapes is presented; for each, the identical shape must be selected from five rotated choices. Fifteen minutes are allowed to complete this test.

Cognitive Abilities

19. Perceptual Speed

Definition: Perceptual speed is the ability to compare letters, numbers, objects, pictures, or patterns, quickly and accurately. The stimuli to be compared may be presented at the same time or in succession. This ability also includes comparing a presented object with a remembered object.

Tasks: Perceptual speed is involved in rapid identification of target aircraft or ships, rapid scanning of text for typographical errors, rapid filing of correspondence by dates, inspecting materials for defects while they are moving on a conveyor belt, locating the batting records of certain players, and scanning the stock market page of the newspaper to check gains and losses of various stocks.

Jobs: Jobs that require high levels of perceptual speed include those of a clerk-typist, maintenance troubleshooter, inspector, post office clerk, telephone operator, and proofreader.

Test Examples: Tests of perceptual speed usually require subjects to scan words or patterns and indicate similarities, differences, or errors. These tests are often used to assess clerical skills.

Finding A's Test—P-1
Educational Testing Service
reprinted by permission of Educational Testing Service, the copyright owner

In this test of perceptual speed, subjects are presented with several columns of words. They are told to draw a line through any word that contains the letter "a." Each of the test's two parts has 820 words. Two minutes are allowed to complete each part. The test has been used in research and experimental applications with students in grades 6 through 16.

Number Comparison—P-2
Educational Testing Service
reprinted by permission of Educational Testing Service, the copyright owner

In this test of perceptual speed, subjects inspect pairs of multi-digit numbers and indicate whether the two numbers in each pair are the same or different. Each part has 48 items and 1.5 minutes are allowed for each part. The test is suitable for grades 6 through 16 and has been used in research and experimental applications.

Cognitive Abilities

20. Selective Attention

Definition: Selective attention is the ability to concentrate on a task over a period of time. This ability involves concentrating while performing a task without being distracted by external stimuli. It involves concentrating on a task and filtering out distractors rather than using information from two or more sources.

Tasks: Selective attention is involved in scanning a display for infrequent targets while alone at night, studying a technical manual in a noisy boiler room, and listening to landing instructions from a control tower while screening out other background conversation.

Jobs: Jobs that require high levels of selective attention include those of an air traffic controller, radio transmitter operator, night watchman, and lifeguard.

Test Examples: No standard tests of selective attention were identified.

Cognitive Abilities

21. Time Sharing

Definition: Time sharing is the ability to shift back and forth efficiently between two or more activities or sources of information. The information can be in the form of speech, signals, sounds, touch, or other sources. This ability involves using information from more than one source rather than concentrating on one task while filtering out distractors.

Tasks: Time sharing is involved when an air traffic controller monitors many targets and signals, a waiter has to deal with many orders at once, a coach has to watch the actions of many team members while giving directions, and a driver has to pay attention to road signs.

Jobs: Jobs that require high levels of time sharing include those of an air traffic controller, radio transmitter operator, sound mixer, waiter/waitress, and athletics coach.

Test Examples: No standard tests of time sharing were identified.

Psychomotor Abilities

22. Control Precision

Definition: Control precision is the ability to make highly controlled and precise adjustments in moving the controls of a machine or vehicle quickly and repeatedly to exact positions. It involves quick or continuous adjustments rather than the timing or rapid choice of movements.

Tasks: Control precision is involved when an astronaut adjusts his/her orbit using a stick control, a dentist drills a tooth, a factory worker turns a valve to match a pressure setting, a truck driver shifts gears, or a pilot makes precise adjustments of his or her rudder pedals.

Jobs: Jobs that require high levels of control precision include those of a sound mixer, pilot, fork lift vehicle operator, bombardier, crane operator, and truck driver.

Test Examples: Tests of control precision usually require subjects to operate an apparatus that involves precise movement of controls in order to achieve a particular status of a given stimulus.

Rotary Pursuit Test
Lafayette Instrument Co, Inc.

This test requires subjects to try to keep a stylus tip in contact with a target set near the edge of a revolving turntable. The score is the total time "on target" during the test period.

Control Adjustment Test
Cited in Fleishman, 1964 and 1972

This test requires subjects to adjust a stick control of the test apparatus to match the indicated positions of stimulus light patterns. The score is the number of matches in the time period.

Psychomotor Abilities

23. Multilimb Coordination

Definition: Multilimb coordination is the ability to coordinate movements of two or more limbs (e.g., two arms, two legs, or one leg and one arm), for example, while moving equipment controls. Two or more limbs are in motion while the individual is sitting, standing, or lying down. This ability does not involve performing these activities while the body is in motion.

Tasks: Multilimb coordination is involved in piloting a plane, playing a drum set in a jazz band, operating a fork-lift truck in a warehouse, and operating a sewing machine with a foot treadle.

Jobs: Jobs that require high levels of multilimb coordination include those of a pilot, drummer, seamstress, orchestra conductor, and race car driver.

Test Examples: Tests of multilimb coordination usually require subjects to manipulate multiple equipment controls with two or more limbs.

Two Arm Coordination Test
Lafayette Instrument Co, Inc.

This is a 1-item performance test. The testing unit consists of a stylus mounted on an apparatus with two handles. The individual grasps both handles simultaneously and moves the stylus around a 6-point star pattern. This test has been used to measure perceptual motor abilities involving the use of both arms together.

Rudder Control Test
Cited in Fleishman, 1964 and 1972

The test unit consists of a cockpit type of apparatus. Subjects are required to coordinate foot pedals to line up the cockpit with target lights. The score is the total time the subject is lined up precisely.

Two-Hand Coordination Test
Cited in Fleishman, 1964 and 1972

The subject stands before a unit situated on a table. The subject grasps the apparatus' two handles which control the movement of a button over a moving target disc. One handle moves the button right and left and the other handle moves it toward and away from the subject. Coordinating these two handles moves the button in any resultant direction. The task is to try to keep this button in contact with the moving target disc as it moves in an eccentric pattern. The score is the subject's "time on target."

Psychomotor Abilities

---

24. Response Orientation

Definition: Response orientation is the ability to choose between two or more movements quickly and correctly when two or more different signals (lights, sounds, pictures) are given. The ability is concerned with the speed with which the correct response can be started with the hand, foot, or other parts of the body. This ability has sometimes been called Choice Reaction Time.

This ability can involve rapid selection of the direction to move a control or which control to move; deciding whether or not to push a button, or hit a pedal, depending on the signals received or the situation encountered.

Tasks: Response orientation is involved when a pilot must decide which controls to move and in which direction, after seeing a light or hearing a sound cue, and when a driver must decide to hit either the brake or gas pedal in a skid situation.

Jobs: Jobs that require high levels of response orientation include those of a race car driver, switch-board operator, and anesthesiologist.

Test Examples: Response orientation tests usually come in the form of choice reaction-time tasks. Subjects are presented with one of several auditory or visual stimuli. Different responses are required depending on the particular stimulus being presented.

Multi-Choice Reaction Time Apparatus
Lafayette Instrument Co., Inc.

This is an apparatus that provides several visual (red, blue, or green) and an auditory (2800 Hz) stimuli. The apparatus also has three telegraph response keys. The experimenter can select one of the four stimuli and one of the three response keys. The time interval between the ready light and stimulus presentation can be varied. Two or more units can be used together for discriminative reaction time (response orientation) tasks.

Psychomotor Abilities

25. Rate Control

Definition: Rate control is the ability to adjust an equipment control in response to changes in the speed and/or direction of a continuously moving object or scene. The ability involves *timing* the adjustments and anticipating changes. This ability does not extend to situations in which both the speed and direction of the object are perfectly predictable.

Tasks: Rate control is involved in tracking a moving aircraft in a gun sight, keeping an airplane at a given altitude in turbulent weather, keeping up with a car one is following when the speed of the first car may vary, riding a bicycle alongside a runner, and hitting a baseball.

Jobs: Jobs that require high levels of rate control include those of a dentist, motion-picture photographer, artillery gunner, baseball player, and truck driver.

Test Examples: Tests of rate control usually require subjects to manipulate controls of test apparatus to keep a variably moving marker in place. The emphasis in these tasks is on timing.

Bassin Anticipation Timer
Lafayette Instrument Co., Inc.

The apparatus for this test consists of a control unit, a start and finish (L.E.D.) lighted runway, and a response push button. The objective of the task is to time your response to coincide with the arrival of a target light at the end of the runway. An adjustable warning light initiates each trial.

Motor Judgment Test
Cited in Fleishman, 1964 and 1972

The apparatus for this test is a box with two rotating discs that are side by side. Portions of each disk are blackened. There is a pointer in the middle of the second disc that moves back and forth. The speed of this pointer is controlled by a lever. Subjects are required to manipulate the speed of the pointer so that it makes as many revolutions as possible without crossing the black areas on the rotating discs.

Single Dimension Pursuit Test
Cited in Fleishman, 1964 and 1972

For this test, subjects are required to manipulate a "dampened" control wheel to keep a line in the window of the apparatus centered as it deviates unpredictably from the center position.

Psychomotor Abilities

26. Reaction Time

Definition: Reaction time is the ability to give a fast response to a signal (sound, light, picture) when it appears. This ability is concerned with the speed with which the movement can be started with the hand, foot, or other parts of the body, but not with the speed with which the movement is carried out once started. It does not involve choosing which response to make. This ability is not measured when more than one type of signal must be discriminated or more than one type of response chosen.

Tasks: Reaction time is involved in firing a weapon as soon as a target appears, hitting the brake when a pedestrian steps in front of the car, hitting back a ball in a ping-pong game, and ducking to miss a snowball thrown at close range.

Jobs: Jobs that include high levels of reaction time include those of a taxicab driver, police officer, combat rifleman, and body guard.

Test Examples: Reaction time tests require subjects to make one specified response as quickly as possible when a visual or auditory stimulus is presented. More accurate measures of reaction time are obtained when subjects are required to keep their hand on the response button or lever rather than move their hand to respond when the stimulus appears. The format in such tests is for a series of such stimuli to be presented. As each stimulus appears, the subject makes his or her response as quickly as possible and waits for the next stimulus. The interval between stimuli may vary so that the subject cannot anticipate the exact time when the next stimulus will appear. Reaction times are accumulated over the test period.

Multi-Choice Reaction Time Apparatus
Lafayette Instrument Co., Inc.

This is an apparatus that provides several visual (red, blue, or green) and an auditory (2800 Hz) stimuli. The apparatus also has three telegraph response keys. The experimenter can select one of the four stimuli and one of the three response keys. Single stimulus and response key units are also available.

Psychomotor Abilities

27. Arm-Hand Steadiness

Definition: Arm-hand steadiness is the ability to keep the hand and arm steady. It includes steadiness while making an arm movement or while holding the arm and hand in one position. This ability does not involve strength or speed, and is not involved in adjusting equipment controls (e.g., levers). However, it can involve using small, light tools.

Tasks: Arm-hand steadiness is involved in cutting facets in a diamond, firing a rifle, threading a needle, lighting a cigarette, and some kinds of welding.

Jobs: Jobs that require high levels of arm-hand steadiness include those of a dentist, paintings restorer, electrologist, watchmaker, gem cutter, and bomb defuser.

Test Examples: Tests of arm-hand steadiness usually require subjects to place or move a stylus in a straight and steady fashion and/or within certain boundaries.

Steadiness Tester—Groove Type
Lafayette Instrument Co., Inc.

This is a multiple-item performance test that requires subjects to move a stylus in a straight line on a frictionless surface. The testing unit consists of adjustable stainless steel plates that form the sides of a progressively narrowing slit.

Steadiness Tester—Hole Type
Lafayette Instrument Co., Inc.

This is a multiple-item performance test that requires subjects to place a stylus in circular holes of varying size. The testing instrument provides nine holes of diminishing size.

Track Tracing Test
Cited in Fleishman, 1964 and 1972

The test unit is a box with a grooved, maze-like pattern. Subjects are required to insert the stylus in the slot and move it slowly and steadily and at arm's length, trying not to hit the sides or back of the slot. The score is the number of times the stylus hits a side during a trial.

Psychomotor Abilities

---

28. Manual Dexterity

Definition: Manual dexterity is the ability to make skillfully coordinated movements with one hand, a hand together with its arm, or two hands in grasping and manipulating objects. The required movement can be to place, move, or assemble objects such as hand tools or blocks. This ability requires the use of the whole hand in using tools, manipulating objects requiring the whole hand, or assembling or fitting objects together. It involves the degree to which these arm–hand movements can be carried out quickly. It does not involve moving machine or equipment controls, such as levers.

Tasks: Manual dexterity is involved in performing open-heart surgery, putting the parts of an engine back together, using tools in making a bookcase, packaging oranges in crates as rapidly as possible, disassembling and assembling a rifle, and tying a necktie.

Jobs: Jobs that require high levels of manual dexterity include those of a surgeon, carpenter, plumber, dog groomer, firearms cleaner, and auto mechanic.

Test Examples: Tests of manual dexterity usually require subjects to assemble and/or disassemble objects (usually containing nuts and bolts, etc.), or to place pegs into holes on a board according to some rule. Written tests that require subjects to mark mazes, checks, or dots as quickly as possible are not good measures of manual dexterity.

Minnesota Manual Dexterity Test
Lafayette Instrument Co., Inc.

The test materials consist of a board with 60 holes arranged in four rows containing 60 round pegs painted red on one side and black on the other. For the first test, subjects transfer pegs (same color up) to the empty board using one hand (finger dexterity). For the second test, the pegs are left in the board and subjects remove each peg, one at a time with one hand, turn it over, transfer it to the other hand, and replace it in the same position on the board until all pegs have been turned. Subjects are allowed 6–10 minutes to complete the test.

Hand-Tool Dexterity Test

The Psychological Corporation

This test requires subjects to take apart twelve assemblies of nuts, bolts, and washers from a wooden frame according to a prescribed sequence and then reassemble them. Seven minutes are allowed to complete the test, which is not suitable for group use. It has been used in selecting applicants for mechanical and industrial jobs.

Stromberg Dexterity Test (STD)

The Psychological Corporation

This is a two-trial performance test that requires subjects to discriminate and sort biscuit-sized discs and to move and place them as fast as possible. The test takes 5–10 minutes to complete and is not suitable for group use. It has been used to select applicants for jobs requiring manual speed and accuracy. It has also been used for assessing manual dexterity of handicapped individuals in vocational training programs.

VCWS8-Simulated Assembly

Valpar International Corporation

This test requires subjects to stand in front of two bins, take parts from each bin, and assemble them. It has been used to measure an individual's ability to work at an assembly task requiring repetitive physical manipulation and bilateral use of the upper extremities. It has also been used to determine standing and sitting tolerance.

Psychomotor Abilities

29. Finger Dexterity

Definition: Finger dexterity is the ability to make skillful, coordinated movements of the fingers of one or both hands and to grasp, place, or move very small objects. This ability involves the degree to which these finger movements can be carried out quickly.

Tasks: Finger dexterity is involved in fixing a watch, assembling small electronic components, and using tweezers.

Jobs: Jobs that require high levels of finger dexterity include those of a dentist, surgeon, electronics assembler, interpreter (deaf), manicurist, make-up artist, jewelry repairer, and seamstress.

Test Examples: Tests of finger dexterity usually require subjects to manipulate small objects with or without tweezers or to assemble small objects or intricate pieces of equipment.

Purdue Pegboard Test
Lafayette Instrument Co., Inc.

This is a multiple-operation manual test of gross- and fine-motor movements of hands, fingers, arms, and tips of fingers. Subjects are required to insert as many pegs as possible into the holes of a pegboard. Normative data are available for a variety of industrial jobs as well as for males and females in general. Subjects are allowed 5-10 minutes to complete the test. It has been used in the selection of business and industrial personnel.

Crawford Small Parts Dexterity Test (CSPDT)
The Psychological Corporation

This is a two-part performance test. Subjects are required to use tweezers to assemble pins and collars, and to screw small screws using a screwdriver after placing them in threaded holes. Subjects are allowed 10-15 minutes to complete the test. It has been used for selecting applicants for such jobs as engraver, watch repairer, and telephone installer.

O'Connor Finger Dexterity Test
Stoelting Co

This is a multiple-operation manual test using a board containing a shallow well, holes (arranged in 10 rows), and a set of 300 pins. Subjects are required to place three pins in each hole. Subects are allowed 8-16 minutes to complete the test. It has been used to determine individual aptitude for small assembly jobs requiring rapid hand work.

O'Connor Tweezer Dexterity Test
Stoelting Co.

This is a multiple-operation manual test using a board containing a shallow well, 100 small holes (arranged in 10 rows), and 100 one-inch pins. Subjects are required to place a pin in each of the holes using only small tweezers. The test takes 8-10 minutes to complete. It has been used to identify vocational aptitude.

Psychomotor Abilities

30. Wrist-Finger Speed

Definition: Wrist-finger speed is the ability to make fast, simple, repeated movements of the fingers, hands, and wrists. It involves little, if any, accuracy or eye-hand coordination. Speed of carrying out a movement is involved rather than starting a movement.

Tasks: Wrist-finger speed is involved in rapidly sending Morse code messages using a manual telegraph key, scrambling eggs with a fork, and using a pencil sharpener.

Jobs: Jobs that require high levels of wrist-finger speed include those of an orchestra conductor, stenographer, typist, butcher, hairdresser, seamstress, and telegrapher.

Test Examples: Tests of wrist-finger speed usually require subjects to tap one object against another as quickly as possible.

Tapping Board
Lafayette Instrument Co., Inc.

This is a multiple-item task-performance test. Subjects are required to tap with a stylus, as rapidly as possible, two stainless steel plates located at each end of an 18-inch fiber-resin board.

Psychomotor Abilities

31. Speed–of–Limb Movement

Definition: Speed–of–limb movement is the ability to quickly execute a single movement of the arms or legs. This ability does not include accuracy, careful control, or coordination of movement. It involves movement of the arms or legs rather than the whole body. It also involves speed in carrying out, rather than starting, a movement.

Tasks: Speed–of–limb movement is involved in reaching for a switch as quickly as possible, quickly moving a control handle from left to right, and moving the foot from the accelerator to the brake pedal to avoid an obstacle.

Jobs: Jobs that require high levels of speed–of–limb movement include those of a race car driver, shoe shiner, and switchboard operator.

Test Examples: Tests of speed–of–limb movement usually require subjects to flip switches or tap objects in an alternating manner as quickly as possible.

Toggle Switch Device
Lafayette Instrument Co., Inc.

The test unit consists of four rows of ten toggle switches. A typical protocol includes recording times required to flip the switches in each row, in all rows, and in all columns.

Two Plate Tapping
Cited in Fleishman, 1964

This test unit is a box with two metal plates placed at least six inches apart. Subjects are required to strike each metal plate, with a stylus, alternately right to left and back, as rapidly as possible. The score is the number of taps during the test period.

Physical Abilities

---

32. Static Strength

Definition: Static strength is the ability to use continuous muscle force in order to lift, push, pull, or carry objects. It is the maximum force that one can exert for a brief period of time using the hand, arm, back, shoulder, or leg.

Static strength does not involve prolonged exertion of the muscles, and involves continuous rather than bursts of muscle force. It involves muscle force against objects rather than muscle power to hold up the body's weight.

Tasks: Static strength is involved in changing a tire on a truck, loading crates on a shelf, pushing open a heavy door, and lifting up a heavy tool box.

Jobs: Jobs that require high levels of static strength include those of a fire fighter, mail carrier, construction worker, shipping clerk, dock worker, bellhop, and ambulance attendant.

Test Examples: Tests of static strength usually are isometric tests which require subjects to grip, push, or pull a test apparatus using full force.

Hand Dynamometer (Dynamometer Grip Strength Test)
Lafayette Instrument Co., Inc.

The apparatus is a millimeter rule and grip dynamometer with stirrups that are adjusted until the inside scale equals half the distance from where the subject's thumb joins the hand to the end of the fingers. Subjects squeeze with full strength, which is measured by the dynamometer. It takes one minute to complete this test. It has been used for vocational evaluation, employee screening, and fitness evaluation.

Jackson Strength Evaluation System
Lafayette Instrument Co., Inc.

The hardware for this system includes a monitor with large LCD readouts that display and hold peak and average force in pounds; a 1000-pound strain gauge load cell; a hand dynamometer fixture; and a sturdy platform, bar and chain assembly. The system comes complete with detailed instructions and norms. It has been used for industrial, pre-employment testing.

Physical Abilities

---

33. Explosive Strength

Definition: Explosive strength is the ability to use short bursts of muscle force to propel oneself or an object. It requires gathering energy for bursts of muscle effort over a very short time period. It involves short bursts of power, rather than continuous use of muscle force.

Tasks: Explosive strength is involved in jumping up onto a platform, jumping across a stream, running 100 yards to catch a thief, throwing a ball as far as possible, throwing a punch, and splitting a log with an ax.

Jobs: Jobs that require high levels of explosive strength include those of a fire fighter, police officer, lifeguard, baseball player, and spear fisher.

Test Examples: Tests of explosive strength usually require subjects to throw an object, to jump, or to sprint.

Vertisonic
Lafayette Instrument Co., Inc.

This is a test apparatus that uses a sonar to objectively measure vertical jumps. Subjects first stand with arm extended upward toward a target string. They then jump upward, reaching for the target string. Sonar waves are used to determine the difference from the standing reach to the jump reach. This provides a measure of lower body explosive strength.

Broad Jump
Cited in Fleishman, 1964

This test is conducted on an indoor mat or an outdoor jump pit. Subjects put their toes up to a start line and then jump as far forward as possible. Before jumping subjects are told to bend their knees. In jumping they simultaneously extend their knees and swing their arms forward. The score is the best jump out of three, as measured from the start line to the rear of the foot closest to the start line at impact. The jump does not count if a subject falls backward.

50-Yard Dash
Cited in Fleishman, 1964

Subjects start with one knee on the ground and fingers on the starting line. They are told, "First take your mark at which you will be ready for the starting commands. Second, get set. With this, raise your body off your haunches and get yourself balanced properly, as far forward as possible, for the start. Do not lean too far forward – you may false start. At the command 'go,' run. Straighten up before you reach the tape, but not immediately if you feel it will slow you down. Most important is to get off your marks as fast as possible." The score is the fastest time for two sprints.

Softball Throw
Cited in Fleishman, 1964

Subjects are required to throw a standard 12-inch softball as far as possible. They are not permitted to run into the throw or shift their feet during the throw. Distance to first bounce is the score. The best of three throws is recorded. This test is typically conducted outdoors on an open field approximately 100 yards long.

Physical Abilities

34. Dynamic Strength

Definition: Dynamic strength is the ability of the muscles to exert force repeatedly or continuously over a long time period. This ability is involved in supporting, holding up, or moving the body's own weight, or objects, repeatedly over time. It represents muscular endurance and emphasizes the resistance of the muscles to fatigue. It does not involve cardiovascular fitness.

Tasks: Dynamic strength is used in climbing a high ladder, climbing a rope using mainly the arms, cutting lumber, climbing a cliff with hammer and pitons, and digging a 50-foot trench in clay soil.

Jobs: Jobs that require high levels of dynamic strength include those of a fire fighter, ditch digger, construction worker, tree cutter, and furnace tender.

Test Examples: Tests of dynamic strength usually require subjects to push or pull one's body against or up to a surface.

Bent-Arm Hang
Cited in Fleishman, 1964

Subjects are required to pull up to a chinning bar until eyebrows are level with the middle of the bar. They are told to keep this position as long as possible.

Pull-ups
Cited in Fleishman, 1964

Subjects are required to hang from a horizontal metal or wooden bar, approximately 1.5 inches in diameter. The bar must be high enough for subjects to hang off the floor with arms and legs fully extended. Subjects are told to grip the bar with palms facing their body. When given the signal to start, they are to pull their body up so that they can set their chin over the bar and then lower their body back to the fully extended position. They are told to do as many pull-ups as possible.

Push-ups
Cited in Fleishman, 1964

Subjects are in a prone position, with hands beside the chest, fingers pointed forward. Hands are to be placed far enough apart so that the forearms make a right angle with the floor. Feet are to be together, body straight, and only chin and chest are allowed to touch the floor. The body is to be raised until the arms are stiff and the back is not to be arched. They are told to do as many push-ups as possible.

Physical Abilities

---

35. Trunk Strength

Definition: Trunk strength is the ability of the stomach and lower back muscles to support part of the body repeatedly or continuously over time. This ability involves the degree to which the muscles in the trunk area do not fatigue when they are put under such repeated or continuous strain.

It involves holding up part, rather than all, of the body, and the degree to which muscles do not give out, rather than the degree to which one does not get winded.

Tasks: Trunk strength is involved in doing sit–ups and leg lifts, using tools while working in a half sit–up position, and removing a heavy piece of equipment while bending over.

Jobs: Jobs that require high levels of trunk strength include those of an auto mechanic, plumber, steel mill worker and carpenter.

Test Examples: Tests of trunk strength usually require subjects to repeatedly or continuously lift part of the body using trunk muscles.

Leg Lifts
Cited in Fleishman, 1964

Subjects are instructed to lie flat on their back with hands clasped behind their neck. A partner should hold their elbows to the ground. The subjects raise their legs to a vertical position, and lower them to the floor as many times as possible and as fast as they can within 30 seconds.

Sit-ups
Cited in Fleishman, 1964

Subjects first lie flat on their back with legs bent and feet shoulder width apart on the floor. They are told to sit up and back down again as many time as possible within a specified time limit.

Physical Abilities

36. Extent Flexibility

Definition: Extent flexibility is the ability to bend, stretch, twist, or reach out with the body, arms, or legs. It involves the *degree* of bending (range of motion) rather than the *speed* of bending.

Tasks: Extent flexibility is involved in working in awkward or cramped positions, performing gymnastics, playing basketball, and in activities requiring reaching.

Jobs: Jobs that require high levels of extent flexibility include those of a window cleaner, warehouse order selector, tree trimmer, auto mechanic, telephone line worker, and petroleum refinery maintenance worker.

Test Examples: Extent flexibility tests usually require subjects to bend, stretch, or twist. The extent, or angle, to which this can be done is measured.

Arthrodial Protractor
Lafayette Instrument Co., Inc.

This measuring device quickly and accurately tests the range of motion for all major joints of the body. Subjects are asked, for example, to reach. The Plexiglass protractor is held up against the reach and the angle is measured.

Flexibility Tester
Lafayette Instrument Co., Inc.

This apparatus is used to measure hip and lower back flexibility. Subjects sit with feet against an aluminum box and flex forward, moving the slide bar with their hands to a point of maximum travel.

Extent Flexibility Test ("Twist and Touch")
Cited in Fleishman, 1964

Subjects are told to stand with left side toward, and at arms length from, a wall. With feet together and in place, they twist back around as far as they can, touching the wall with their right hand at shoulder height.

Physical Abilities

37. Dynamic Flexibility

Definition: Dynamic flexibility is the ability to bend, stretch, twist, or reach out with the body, arms or legs, both quickly and repeatedly. It involves both speed and repeated bending or stretching as well as the degree to which muscles "bounce back" during these repeated activities.

Tasks: Dynamic flexibility is involved in swimming the butterfly stroke, shoveling coal into a furnace, and filling a bag with shells at the seashore.

Jobs: Jobs that require high levels of dynamic flexibility include those of a flower picker, fruit harvest worker, gardener, and dry-wall applicator.

Test Examples: Tests of dynamic flexibility usually require subjects to perform multiple bending, stretching, and twisting movements.

Stability Testing and Rehabilitation Station
Lafayette Instrument Co., Inc.

This apparatus uses a modification of the Biomechanic Ankle Platform System design which has been used to restore ankle flexibility and strength. The unit measures and records ankle strength, stability, and flexibility.

Dynamic Flexibility Test ("Bend, Twist, & Touch")
Cited in Fleishman, 1964

With their back to the wall and hands together, subjects bend forward, touch an "X" between their feet, straighten, twist to the left and touch an "X" behind them on the wall. The cycle is repeated, alternately twisting to the right and to the left, doing as many as possible in the time allowed.

Physical Abilities

38. Gross Body Coordination

Definition: Gross body coordination is the ability to coordinate the movement of the arms, legs, and torso in activities in which the whole body is
in motion. It is not involved in coordinating arms and legs while the body
is at rest.

Tasks: Gross body coordination is involved in performing a skilled ballet
dance, parachuting from an airplane, completing an obstacle course (with no
time limit), diving, and swimming.

Jobs: Jobs that require high levels of gross body coordination include those
of a dancer, scuba diver, basketball player, and tree trimmer.

Test Examples: Tests of gross body coordination require subjects to coordinate different parts of the body while executing a movement of the entire
body.

Cable Jump Test
Cited in Fleishman, 1964

Subjects are told to hold a short jump rope in front of them, one end
in either hand. They must attempt to jump through this rope without
tripping, falling, or releasing the rope.

Physical Abilities

39. Gross Body Equilibrium

Definition: Gross body equilibrium is the ability to keep or regain one's balance or to stay upright when in an unstable position. This ability includes maintaining one's balance when changing direction, either while moving or standing motionless. It does not include balancing objects.

Tasks: Gross body equilibrium is involved in walking on narrow beams in high-rise construction, working on a telephone pole, walking on a rolling deck, riding a surfboard, walking on ice across a pond, and standing on a ladder.

Jobs: Jobs that require high levels of gross body equilibrium include those of a ballet dancer, gymnast, fire fighter, power line repair person, and construction worker.

Test Examples: Gross body equilibrium tests usually require subjects to balance on a platform or beam, generally with eyes closed.

Basic Balance Beam
Lafayette Instrument Co., Inc.

Subjects are required to balance, using the preferred foot, for as long as possible on a beam.

Rail Walking
From Fleishman, 1964

Subjects are required to walk along a narrow rail, for as long as possible, without falling off.

Physical Abilities

40. Stamina

Definition: Stamina is the ability of the lungs and circulatory systems of the body to perform efficiently over long time periods. This is the ability to exert oneself physically over long periods without getting out of breath. The heart rate goes up significantly during activities requiring this ability. It involves not getting "winded" rather than not fatiguing the muscles.

Tasks: Stamina is involved in running long distances, cross-country skiing, mountain climbing, performing calisthenics for half an hour, swimming long distances, and riding a bicycle.

Jobs: Jobs that require high levels of stamina include those of a fire fighter, scuba diver, mountain trail guide, delivery person (bicycle or on-foot), and mail carrier.

Test Examples: Stamina tests usually require subjects to perform an exercise using maximum effort over a prolonged period of time.

Fitness Equipment 5000 Treadmill Test
Lafayette Instrument, Inc.

Subjects are required to continue to walk on a treadmill at a given pace until they slow below a critical point.

Step Test
Cited in Cotten, 1971

Subjects are required to stand in front of a bench (13 to 20 inches in height). They are told to place one foot on the bench and step up until both feet are fully on the bench, then step down one foot at a time. The pace is counted off by the administrator. The score is derived from the heart rate after 5–10 minutes of performance.

600-Yard Run-Walk Test or Mile Run
Cited in Fleishman, 1964

Subjects are required to cover a 600-yard distance in as short a time as possible. Recent modifications for adults have included a one mile run or distance covered in 12 minutes.

Sensory/Perceptual Abilities

41. Near Vision

Definition: Near vision is the capacity to see close environmental surroundings. It is the ability to see details of objects, numbers, letters, designs, or pictures within a few feet of the observer. These details should be in sharp focus. Deficits in near vision are associated with the visual acuity impairment of myopia (farsightedness).

Tasks: Near vision is involved in reading books, manuals or plans, watching a computer monitor, inspecting products for defects, looking through microscopes, and watching gauges and instruments on control panels.

Jobs: Jobs that require high levels of near vision include those of a maintenance trouble shooter, microbiologist, electrician, watch repairer, proofreader, secretary, meter reader, medical technician, and draftsman.

Test Examples: Tests of near vision usually require subjects to read letters or numbers on a chart. The distance from which subjects can read the chart is compared with that of a person with normal vision. The standard distance for near vision is 14 inches. Vision charts for those who cannot read English are also available. Tests of near vision are often administered using a telebinocular apparatus.

Visual Skills Test Set
Keystone View, Division of Mast Development Co.

Using telebinocular equipment, subjects are presented a slide with balls arranged in a circle. On the balls are either lines, dots, or gray shading. Subjects are instructed to identify which pattern is on each of the balls. Similar tests are provided for monocular acuity (DB 16 and DB 17).

Visual Survey Telebinocular (Vision Screening Telebinocular)
Keystone View, Division of Mast Development Co.

Subjects are asked specific questions about slides that are presented to them via telebinocular equipment. Responses are scored to determine near and far acuity.

Titmus II Vision Tester: Professional Model
Titmus Optical, Inc./Stereo Optical Co

Subjects are asked to respond to eight slides presented via a vision tester. Responses are scored to determine near and far acuity, as well as color vision.

Sensory/Perceptual Abilities

42. Far Vision

Definition: Far vision is the capacity to see distant environmental surroundings. It is the ability to see details of objects at a distance. Deficits in far vision are associated with the visual acuity impairment of presbyopia (nearsightedness).

Tasks: Far vision is involved in seeing street signs while driving a car, standing watch on a ship deck, bird watching, and seeing the numbers on the jerseys of football players while sitting in the stands.

Jobs: Jobs that require high levels of far vision include those of an astronomer, surveyor, ship captain, and combat rifleman.

Test Examples: Tests of far vision usually require subjects to read letters or numbers on a chart. The distance from which subjects can read the chart is compared with that of a person with normal vision. The standard distance for testing far vision is 20 feet. Vision ability is expressed as a ratio comparing the distance at which a normal person sees an object to the distance at which the subject sees the object. Thus, 20/20 indicates normal vision while 20/15 indicates above average vision and 20/30 indicates below average vision. Vision charts for those who cannot read English are also available.

Far Point Landolt Ring Acuity Test
Keystone View, Division of Mast Development Co.

This is an alternative to the Snellen Chart. Subjects view rings with gaps of varying sizes. Subjects indicate which rings appear whole and which appear to have a gap. The size of the ring for which the smallest gap is perceived is compared with normative standards to determine the subjects' far acuity. Keystone View presents this test via telebinocular equipment.

Far Point Snellen Letter Acuity Test
Keystone View, Division of Mast Development Co.

The traditional Snellen test consists of a chart of rows of letters. The top row is the largest and subsequent rows are progressively smaller. Subjects are required to stand 20 feet from the chart and read the smallest row possible. Results are compared to standards for what a person with normal vision sees at 20 feet and presented in the form of a fraction (described above). Keystone View has adapted this test so that it can be administered via telebinocular equipment.

Far Point "Tumbling E" Acuity Test
Keystone View, Division of Mast Development Co.

Also known as the "illiterate E" test, this is an alternative to the
Snellen Chart which does not require any reading ability. Subjects
view Es of varying sizes. They indicate the visibility of the letter by
indicating the direction of each E with their hand. Keystone View
presents this test via telebinocular equipment.

Usable Vision Binocular—DB-1D
Keystone View, Division of Mast Development Co.

Subjects are presented slides via telebinocular equipment. The slides
contain five white squares at various distances. They are required to
indicate in which corner of each square a black dot is located. This
test is designed to avoid confounds of the Snellen Chart due to
recognition of familiar contours. Also, while the Snellen Chart
measures maximum acuity, these cards provides a measure of the
habitual performance of each eye. Thus, this test is better designed to
identify a functional loss of vision.

Sensory/Perceptual Abilities

43. Visual Color Discrimination

Definition: Visual color discrimination is the capacity to match or discriminate between colors. This capacity also includes detecting differences in color purity (saturation) and brightness (brilliance).

Tasks: Visual color discrimination is involved in tracing wire circuits in which the wires are color-coded, discriminating between light signals of different colors, painting a portrait, and matching wood grains in a lumber yard.

Jobs: Jobs that require high levels of visual color discrimination include those of an interior designer, chemist, electrician, house painter, color tester, graphics designer, fabric colormaker, chemist, and cosmetics supervisor.

Test Examples: Tests of near vision require subjects to complete tasks that demonstrate an ability to distinguish between hues. These tasks might involve categorizing, identifying, or ordering objects or shapes.

Ishihara Test for Color Blindness
Lafayette Instrument Co., Inc.

This test requires subjects to respond to pseudo-isochromatic plates. These plates consist of dots of different colors arranged so that a person with normal color vision perceives a numeral. A person with a color vision deficiency will perceive only dots. Protan and deutan color deficiencies can be identified with this test. This test consists of 24 items, takes less than one minute to complete, and is suitable for group administration.

Dvorine Color Vision Test
The Psychological Corporation

This test requires subjects to respond to pseudo-isochromatic plates. They are instructed to read numbers in the plates and trace paths consisting of multicolored dots presented against a background of contrasting dots. The test consists of 15 items with 8 auxiliary plates for verification. It takes 2-3 minutes to administer.

Farnsworth Dichotomous Test for Color Blindness
The Psychological Corporation

This test presents subjects with a hinged rack and different colored caps. One cap is permanently mounted. Subjects are required to arrange the caps on the rack according to color. The pattern of responses is compared to that of individuals with normal color vision. The test takes five minutes to administer.

Sensory/Perceptual Abilities

---

44. Night Vision

Definition: Night vision is the ability to see under low light conditions. It is related to the physiological function of dark adaptation, the process by which the visual system adjusts to reduction in ambient illumination. Since the color receptors of the eye do not function under low illumination, tasks that require high levels of night vision cannot also require high levels of color discrimination.

Tasks: Night vision is involved when developing film in a darkroom, driving at night, standing watch on a ship at night, recognizing someone in an open field at night, and taking notes during a slide presentation.

Jobs: Jobs that require high levels of night vision include those of an astronomer, photographer, night watchman, truck driver, and scuba diver.

Test Examples: Tests of night vision require subjects to respond to or identify stimuli in a simulated night vision environment. No standard tests of night vision were identified.

Sensory/Perceptual Abilities

45. Peripheral Vision

Definition: Peripheral vision is the ability to perceive objects or movement located in the edges of the visual field. Since the periphery of the retina contains fewer vision receptors, vision in the periphery is rather gross and limited to the detection of movement or large stimuli.

Tasks: Peripheral vision is involved in tasks that require visual awareness of objects in the periphery, including driving a car, piloting a plane, marching in formation, and playing basketball.

Jobs: Jobs that require high levels of peripheral vision include those of an astronomer, fighter pilot, basketball player, and taxicab driver.

Test Examples: Tests of peripheral vision usually require subjects to stare straight ahead at a screen and indicate whether or not they perceive stimuli that are being flashed in their periphery.

Field Analyzer
Allergan-Humphries

The Field Analyzer is a device that contains a microprocessor to record test data and provide a visual field map. Subjects are required to look at a central spot on the screen while lights of different intensities are projected inside a large bowl. If they see the light, they indicate this by pressing a button.

Wayne Saccadic Fixator
Wayne Engineering

This apparatus consists of a light panel that is used to present visual stimuli to the subject. For peripheral vision testing, the subject responds to stimuli that are presented in the peripheral field.

Sensory/Perceptual Abilities

46. Depth Perception

Definition: Depth perception is the ability to distinguish which of several objects is more distant from or nearer to the observer, or to judge the distance of an object from the observer. Depth perception has a strong learned component that involves using cues in the environment to determine depth.

Tasks: Depth perception is involved in operating a construction crane, deciding when it is safe to pass a car in the face of oncoming traffic, estimating whether or not two aircraft are on a collision course, and threading a needle.

Jobs: Jobs that require high levels of depth perception include those of a crane operator, truck driver, pilot, and artillery gunner.

Test Examples: Tests of depth perception usually involve the presentation of pictures of objects (often projected onto a screen). Subjects are required to indicate which figure stands out or which is further away.

Stereopsis—DB-6D
Keystone View, Division of Mast Development Co.

Subjects view a slide presented via telebinocular equipment. The slide consists of rows, each containing a star, square, cross, heart, and ball. Subjects are required to indicate for each row which figure seems to be closer than the others. Failure on any portion of this "screen-out" test indicates a need for corrective attention. More exact information is obtained using Keystone's Stereometric Units DC1-23, DC31-53, or Multi-Stereo Tests.

Depth Perception Apparatus
Lafayette Instrument Co., Inc.

This apparatus consists of two adjustable vertical rods housed in a wooden case. The case is designed to eliminate depth cues so that subjects must rely on visual perception only. They are required to indicate which rod is closer than the other.

Randot Stereopsis Test
Titmus Optical, Inc./Stereo Optical Co.

This test presents vectographs (dot patterns on a homogeneous background) that are viewed through Polaroid glasses. Subjects are required to identify the pattern formed by the dots.

Sensory/Perceptual Abilities

47. Glare Sensitivity

Definition: Glare sensitivity is the ability to see objects in the presence of glare or bright ambient lighting.

Tasks: Glare sensitivity is involved when watching swimmers on a sunny day, identifying ships on the horizon, and snow skiing in bright sunlight.

Jobs: Jobs that require high levels of glare sensitivity include those of a bus driver, surveyor, fisherman, and Navy midshipman.

Test Examples: Tests of glare sensitivity require subjects to identify stimuli presented in varying conditions of glare.

Multivision Contrast Tester (MCT) 8000
Visitech Consultants, Inc.

Subjects are required to look into the MCT 8000 apparatus and identify contrast sensitivity stimuli that are presented with an internal slide mechanism. The contrast sensitivity targets are sine-wave gratings which vary among five different spatial frequencies — a procedure with demonstrated ability to quantify visual performance and detect various types of visual problems. Additionally, the apparatus allows three different types of glare to be independently manipulated: central, peripheral, and radial glare. The central glare test simulates a point source of glare such as that from an oncoming automobile headlight at night. This test has been used to estimate visual performance as it relates to performing tasks such as nighttime driving. The MCT 8000 provides standardized calibration along with normative information. Also available from Vistech Consultants, Inc. are disposable, individual pass/fail vision screening tests that are based on the visual targets used in the MCT 8000.

Sensory/Perceptual Abilities

48. Hearing Sensitivity

Definition: Hearing sensitivity is the ability to detect and to discriminate among sounds that vary over broad ranges of pitch and/or loudness. It is thought to be a broad scope ability that underlies the more specific hearing abilities of auditory attention, sound localization, and speech recognition.

Tasks: Hearing sensitivity is involved in detecting targets through sonar operations, receiving Morse code under poor reception conditions, listening for radio signals during a rescue mission, discriminating among the sounds of instruments performing in a symphony, and monitoring electronic equipment at a nurses' station.

Jobs: Jobs that require high levels of hearing sensitivity include those of a nurse, music critic, acoustics engineer, and sonar operator.

Test Examples: Tests of hearing sensitivity usually involve presenting a pure tone signal at varying intensities via an electrical apparatus called an audiometer. The test determines the lowest level than can be detected fifty percent of the time. The subjects "hearing threshold level" for pure tones is then compared to normative information from persons with normal hearing sensitivity. The standard technique (recommended by the American Speech Language Hearing Association and the American National Standards Institute) is called the Modified Hughson-Westlake Technique for Threshold Search. This technique is called a *method of limits* test because the person administering the test adjusts the signal. An alternative method called the *method of adjustment* requires subjects to adjust the signal.

Seashore Measures of Musical Talents
The Psychological Corporation

Six tests are administered via record or reel-to-reel tape. Subjects are tested for their ability to discriminate signals differing in pitch, loudness, time, timbre, rhythm, and for tonal memory. This test takes approximately one hour to complete.

Sensory/Perceptual Abilities

49. Auditory Attention

Definition: Auditory attention is the ability to focus on a single source of auditory information in the presence of other distracting and irrelevant auditory stimuli.

Tasks: Auditory attention is involved in receiving Morse code in a noisy room, and listening for flight announcements at an airport.

Jobs: Jobs that require high levels of auditory attention include those of an auctioneer, bartender, Wall Street stock bidder, and sonar operator.

Test Examples: Tests of auditory attention usually require subjects to identify sounds amidst background noise that are presented via tape recorder.

Code Distraction Task
Cited in Fleishman & Friedman, 1957a, 1957b

Subjects are required to identify Morse code auditory signals consisting of dots and dashes. These signals are presented in the presence of background noise. The background noise consists of signals being sent at a rapid rate. In addition, other noises are presented, such as a door slamming or outside traffic sounds.

Sensory/Perceptual Abilities

---

50. Sound Localization

Definition: Sound localization is the ability to identify the direction from which an auditory stimulus originated relative to the observer. Hearing in both ears facilitates sound localization. Cues that are used to localize sound include distance, intensity, and head movements.

Tasks: Sound localization is involved in tracing the source of noise in a car, setting the balance control on a stereo system, locating someone calling for help in the midst of a crowd, and finding a ringing telephone in a unfamiliar apartment.

Jobs: Jobs that require high levels of sound localization include that of an orchestra conductor, auto mechanic, and lifeguard.

Test Examples: No standard tests of sound localization were identified.

Sensory/Perceptual Abilities

51. Speech Recognition

Definition: Speech recognition is the ability to identify and understand the speech of another person. These stimuli are complex at the acoustic level, due to the sequential and parallel transmission characteristics of a speech signal. Speech recognition also involves cognitive processing. Speech recognition differs from hearing sensitivity in that the stimuli are always loud enough to hear.

Tasks: Speech recognition is involved in understanding oral instructions, identifying a spoken foreign language, recognizing a person's voice, understanding someone with a heavy foreign accent, and understanding someone with a speech impediment.

Jobs: Jobs that require high levels of speech recognition include those of an interpreter, air traffic controller, telephone operator, and auctioneer.

Test Examples: Speech recognition tests typically present subjects with a signal which is barely audible. Subjects are tested for how much of the message they can recognize or follow. These tests generally use monosyllabic words to avoid redundancy. Some use nonsense syllables in order to detect absolute semantic recognition. Tests are either administered in quiet rooms to measure maximum performance or in rooms with background noise to measure everyday performance.

Speech recognition tests differ from tests of hearing sensitivity in that the signals are presented at a high enough level to hear. These tests are designed instead to detect hearing difficulties due to distorted processing in the auditory system.

Lindamood Auditory Conceptualization Test (LAC)
DLM Teaching Resources

This is a 40-item performance response test that requires subjects to arrange colored blocks (each symbolizing one speech sound) in a row to represent a sound pattern spoken by the examiner. The color of each block indicates one speech sound. Repeated sounds in the pattern are symbolized by the same color block and different sounds by different colors.

Wichita Auditory Fusion Test (WAFT)
Modern Education Corporation

This test requires subjects to respond to variations in frequency, intensity, and temporal patterns that comprise the speech signal. These tones are presented via audiotape and earphones.

Tree/Bee Test of Auditory Discrimination (Tree/Bee Test)
United Educational Services, Inc.

This test presents subjects with a series of pictures. The examiner speaks a word or phrase and subjects are required to point to or mark the appropriate picture. This test takes 10 minutes to complete.

Sensory/Perceptual Abilities

52. Speech Clarity

Definition: Speech clarity is the ability to communicate orally in a clear fashion that is understandable to a listener. This ability refers to the diction, syntactic construction, and correct semantic usage by a speaker rather than the breadth of the speaker's vocabulary.

Tasks: Speech clarity is involved in presenting a financial status report to an executive board, presenting a briefing at a press conference, and giving a lecture.

Jobs: Jobs that require high levels of speech clarity include those of an actor, singer, newscaster, air traffic controller, teacher/professor, dispatcher, and telephone operator.

Test Examples: Tests of speech clarity usually assess subjects' speech by requiring them to orally identify pictures, repeat sentences, or read sentences or paragraphs.

Test of Minimal Articulation Competence (T-MAC)
The Psychological Corporation

This test has a flexible format that requires subjects to either identify pictures, read sentences, or repeat sentences. Measures of articulation are obtained for 24 consonant phonemes, frequently occurring "s," "r," and "l" blends, 12 vowels, 4 diphthongs, and variations of vocalic "r." The test takes 10 minutes to complete.

Section II

*Summary of
Representative Tests
for Each Ability*

Cognitive Abilities

1. Oral Comprehension Tests

Test	Author	Publisher
Listening for Meaning Enterprises	Brimer, M. A.	Educational Evaluation
The PSI Basic Skills Tests for Business, Industry, and Government: Following Oral Directions (BST #7)	Ruch, W. W. Shub, A. N. Moinat, S. M. Dye, D. A.	Psychological Services, Inc.
Office Skills Test: Oral Directions	Science Research Associates	Science Research Associates
Watson-Barker Listening Test	Watson, K. W. Barker, L. L.	SPECTRA Communication Associates

2. Written Comprehension Tests

Test	Author	Publisher
Guilford-Zimmerman Aptitude Survey: Verbal Comprehension	Guilford, J. P. Zimmerman, W. S.	Consulting Psychologists Press
Schaie-Thurstone Adult Mental Abilities Test: Verbal	Schaie, K. W.	Consulting Psychologists Press
Advanced Vocabulary Test I – V4	not provided	Educational Testing Service
Advanced Vocabulary Test II – V5	not provided	Educational Testing Service
Extended Range Vocabulary Test	not provided	Educational Testing Service
Vocabulary I	not provided	Educational Testing Service

Vocabulary II	not provided	Educational Testing Service
Job Effectiveness Prediction Verbal Comprehension (JEPS: Test Code H)	Personnel Decisions Research	Institute for Life Office System: Management Association
Understanding Communication	Thurstone, T. G.	London House Press
Reading, Comprehension, Grammar Usage and Structure, and Vocabulary Tests	McCartney, W. A.	William A. McCartney
High Level Battery B/75	not provided	National Institute for Personnel Research
Occupational Aptitude Survey: Reading Comprehension, Vocabulary	Parker, R. M.	Pro-Ed
Industrial Reading Test (IRT)	not provided	The Psychological Corporation
Employee Aptitude Survey Test #1— Verbal Comprehension (EAS #1)	Grimsley, G. Ruch, F. L. Warren, N. D. Ford, J. S.	Psychological Services, Inc.
Professional Employment Test: Verbal Comprehension	not provided	Psychological Services, Inc.
The PSI Basic Skills Tests for Business, Industry and Government: Reading Comprehension (BST #2)	Ruch, W. W. Shub, A. N. Moinat, S. M. Dye, D. A	Psychological Services, Inc.
The PSI Basic Skills Tests for Business, Industry and Government: Following Written Directions (BST #8)	Ruch, W. W. Shub, A. N. Moinat, S. M. Dye, D. A.	Psychological Services, Inc.
Multidimensional Aptitude Battery: Information and Comprehension, Vocabulary	Jackson, D. N.	Research Psychologists Press, Inc.

Reading Comprehension	Richardson, Bellows, Henry, & Co, Inc.	Richardson, Bellows, Henry & Co., Inc.
Nelson–Denny Reading Test: Forms E & F	Brown, J. I. Bennett, J. M. Hanna, G. S.	The Riverside Publishing Co.
Advanced Test Battery: Verbal Concepts (ATB:VA1)	Saville & Holdsworth, Ltd.	Saville & Holdsworth, Ltd.
Technical Test Battery: Verbal Comprehension (TTB:VTI)	Saville & Holdsworth, Ltd.	Saville & Holdsworth, Ltd.
Work Aptitude: Profile and Practice Set: Using Words	Saville & Holdsworth, Ltd.	Saville & Holdsworth, Ltd.
Work Skills Series: Understanding Instructions	Saville & Holdsworth, Ltd.	Saville & Holdsworth, Ltd.
Flanagan Aptitude Classification Tests (FACT): Expression	Flanagan, J. C.	Science Research Associates
Flanagan Industrial Tests (FIT): Expression, Vocabulary	Flanagan, J. C.	Science Research Associates
MD5 Mental Ability Test: Comprehension, Vocabulary/Semantic Relationships	Mackenzie Davey & Co.	The Test Agency
ASVAB: Paragraph Comprehension, Word Knowledge	Department of Defense	U.S. Department of Defense

3. Oral Expression Tests

No standard tests of oral expression were identified.

4. Written Expression Tests

Test	Author	Publisher
Associational Fluency	Christensen, P. R. Guilford, J. P	Consulting Psychologists Press
Expressional Fluency	Christensen, P. R. Guilford, J. P.	Consulting Psychologists Press
Schaie-Thurstone Adult Mental Ability Test: Word Fluency	Schaie, K. W.	Consulting Psychologists Press
Word Fluency	Christensen, P. R. Guilford, J. P.	Consulting Psychologists Press
The Ennis-Weir Critical Thinking Essay Test	Poteet, J. A.	Critical Thinking Press and Software, formerly Midwest Publications
Cooperative English Tests	Educational Testing Service	CTB/McGraw Hill, Inc.
Morrisby Differential Test Battery: Word Fluency	Morrisby, J. B.	Educational and Industrial Test Services, Ltd.
Word Beginnings	not provided	Educational Testing Service
Word Beginnings and Endings	not provided	Educational Testing Service
Word Endings	not provided	Educational Testing Service
Comprehensive Ability Battery: Production of Ideas, Verbal Fluency	Hakstian, A. R.	Institute for Personality and Ability Testing
Word Fluency	Human Resources Center, The University of Chicago	London House Press
Employee Aptitude Survey Test #8— Word Fluency (EAS #8)	Grimsley, G. Ruch, F. L. Warren, N. D. Ford, J. S.	Psychological Services, Inc.

5. Fluency of Ideas Tests

Test	Author	Publisher
Ball Aptitude Battery: Idea Fluency	Sung, Y. H. Dares, R. V.	The Ball Foundation
Alternate Uses	Christensen, P. R. Guilford, J. P. Merrifield, P. R. Wilson, R. C.	Consulting Psychologists Press
Consequences	Christensen, P. R. Merrifield, P. R. Guilford, J. P.	Consulting Psychologists Press
Ideational Fluency	Christensen, P. R. Guilford, J. P.	Consulting Psychologists Press
Morrisby Differential Test Battery: Ideational Fluency	Morrisby, J. B.	Educational and Industrial Test Services, Ltd.
Theme Test	not provided	Educational Testing Service
Thing Categories	not provided	Educational Testing Service
Topics Test—F-1	not provided	Educational Testing Service

6. Originality

Test	Author	Publisher
Consequences	Christensen, P. R. Merrifield, P. R. Guilford, J. P.	Consulting Psychologists Press
Comprehensive Ability Battery: Originality	Hakstian, A. R. Cattell, R. B.	Institute for Personality and Ability Testing, Inc.
Flanagan Aptitude Classification Tests (FACT): Ingenuity	Flanagan, J. C.	Science Research Associates
Flanagan Industrial Tests (FIT): Ingenuity	Flanagan, J. C.	Science Research Associates

7. Memorization Tests

Test	Author	Publisher
Auditory Letter Span Test—MS-3	Kelly, H. P.	Educational Testing Service
Auditory Number Span Test—MS-1	Kelly, H. P.	Educational Testing Service
Building Memory—MV-2	not provided	Educational Testing Service
First & Last Names Test—MA#	not provided	Educational Testing Service
Map Memory—MV-3	not provided	Educational Testing Service
Object-Number Test—MA-2	not provided	Educational Testing Service
Picture-Number Test—MAI	not provided	Educational Testing Service
Shape Memory Test—MV-1	not provided	Educational Testing Service
Visual Number Span Test—MS-2	Kelly, H. P.	Educational Testing Service
Comprehensive Ability Battery: Rote Memory	Hakstian, A. R. Cattell, R. B.	Institute for Personality and Ability Testing, Inc.
Benton Revised Visual Retention Test	Benton, A.	The Psychological Corporation
The PSI Basic Skills Test for Business, Industry, and Government: Memory (BST #16)	Ruch, W. W. Shub, A. N. Moinat, S. M. Dye, D. A.	Psychological Services, Inc.
Flanagan Aptitude Classification Tests (FACT): Memory	Flanagan, J. C.	Science Research Associates
Flanagan Industrial Tests (FIT): Memory	Flanagan, J. C.	Science Research Associates
Shordone-Hall Memory Battery	Shordone, R. J. Hall, S.	Shordone, R. J.

Knox's Cube Test	Stone, M. H. Wrights, R. D.	Stoelting Co.
Project A (U.S. Army): Memory Test, Number Memory Test	cited in Olson (1990)	

---

8. Problem Sensitivity Tests

No standard tests of problem sensitivity were identified.

---

9. Mathematical Reasoning Tests

Test	Author	Publisher
Admissions Examinations: Admissions and Credentialing Group, Doppelt Mathematical Reasoning Test	Doppelt, J. E.	Admissions and Credentialing Group/The Psychological Corporation
Ball Aptitude Battery: Numerical Reasoning	Sung, Y. G. Dares, R. V.	The Ball Foundation
Guilford-Zimmerman Aptitude Survey: General Reasoning	Guilford, J. P. Zimmerman, W. S.	Consulting Psychologists Press
Mathematics Aptitude Test—RG-2	not provided	Educational Testing Service
Necessary Arithmetic Operations—RG-3	not provided	Educational Testing Service
Wonderlic Personnel Test: Numerical Reasoning	Wonderlic, E. F.	E.F. Wonderlic Personnel Test, Inc.
Job Effectiveness Prediction System: Mathematical Skill (JEPS): Test Code C	Personnel Decisions Research Institute for Life Office Management Association	Life Office Management Association

Graduate and Managerial Assessment: Numerical	The Hatfield Polytechnic	NFER-Nelson Publishing Co., Ltd.
Differential Aptitude Test: Numerical Reasoning	Bennett, G. K. Seashore, H. G. Wesman, A. G.	The Psychological Corporation
Professional Employment Test: Quantitative Problem Solving	not provided	Psychological Services, Inc.
The PSI Basic Skills Tests for Business, Industry, and Government: Problem Solving (BST #5)	Ruch, W. W. Shub, A. N. Moinat, S. M. Dye, D. A.	Psychological Services, Inc.
Multidimensional Aptitude Battery: Arithmetic Similarities	Jackson, D. N.	Research Psychologists Press, Inc.
Advanced Test Battery: Number Series (ATB:NA2)	Saville & Holdsworth, Ltd.	Saville & Holdsworth, Ltd.
Technical Test Battery: Numerical Reasoning (TTB:NT6)	Saville & Holdsworth, Ltd.	Saville & Holdsworth, Ltd.
Flanagan Aptitude Classification Tests (FACT): Reasoning	Flanagan, J. C.	Science Research Associates
Flanagan Industrial Tests (FIT): Mathematics and Reasoning	Flanagan, J. C.	Science Research Associates
MD5 Mental Ability Test: Math Relationships	Mackenzie Davey & Co.	The Test Agency
ASVAB: Arithmetic Reasoning	Department of Defense	U.S. Department of Defense

10. Number Facility Tests

Test	*Author*	*Publisher*
Ball Aptitude Battery: Numerical Computation	Sung, Y. H. Dares, R. V.	The Ball Foundation

Guilford–Zimmerman Aptitude Survey: Numerical Operations	Guilford, J. P. Zimmerman, W. S.	Consulting Psychologists Press
Schaie–Thurstone Adult Mental Abilities Test: Number	Schaie, K. W.	Consulting Psychologists Press
Addition and Subtraction Correction	not provided	Educational Testing Service
Addition Test—N-1	not provided	Educational Testing Service
Applied Arithmetic Placement Test	not provided	Educational Testing Service
Division Test	not provided	Educational Testing Service
Subtraction and Multiplication	not provided	Educational Testing Service
Comprehensive Ability Battery: Numerical Ability	Hakstian, A. R. Cattell, R. B.	Institute for Personality & Ability Testing, Inc.
Job Effectiveness Prediction System: Numerical Ability-1 (JEPS:Test Code A)	Personnel Decisions Research Institute for Life Office Management Association	Life Office Management Association
Differential Aptitude Test: Numerical Ability	Bennett, G. K. Seashore, H. G. West, A. G.	The Psychological Corporation
Employee Aptitude Survey #2 Numerical Ability (EAS #2)	Grimsley, G. Warren, N. D.	Psychological Services, Inc.
The PSI Basic Skills Tests for Business, Industry, and Government: Computation (BST #4)	Ruch, W. W. Shub, A. N. Moinat, S. M. Dye, D. A.	Psychological Services, Inc.
Arithmetic Fundamentals	Richardson, Bellows, Henry & Co., Inc.	Richardson, Bellows, Henry & Co., Inc.
Shop Arithmetic Test	Richardson, Bellows, Henry & Co., Inc.	Richardson, Bellows, Henry & Co., Inc.

Automated Office Battery: Numerical Estimation (AOB:NE-1)	Saville & Holdsworth, Ltd.	Saville & Holdsworth, Ltd.
Technical Test Battery: Numerical Computation (TTB:NT2)	Saville & Holdsworth, Ltd.	Saville & Holdsworth, Ltd.
Work Aptitude Profile and Practice Set: Being Accurate	Saville & Holdsworth, Ltd.	Saville & Holdsworth, Ltd.
Work Skills Series: Working With Numbers	Saville & Holdsworth, Ltd.	Saville & Holdsworth, Ltd.
Flanagan Aptitude Classification Tests (FACT): Arithmetic Ability	Flanagan, J. C.	Science Research Associates
Flanagan Industrial Tests (FIT): Arithmetic Ability	Flanagan, J. C.	Science Research Associates
Office Skills Test: Numerical Skills	Science Research Associates	Science Research Associates
SRA Reading-Arithmetic Index	Science Research Associates	Science Research Associates
Short Tests of Clerical Ability (STCA)	Science Research Associates	Science Research Associates
MD5 Mental Ability Test: Math Procedures	Mackenzie Davey & Co.	The Test Agency
ASVAB: Numerical Operations	Department of Defense	U.S. Department of Defense

11. Deductive Reasoning Tests

Test	Author	Publisher
Deciphering Languages	not provided	Educational Testing Service
Diagramming Relationships	not provided	Educational Testing Service
Inference Test	not provided	Educational Testing Service

Nonsense Syllogisms— RL-1	not provided	Educational Testing Service
Differential Aptitude Test: Verbal Reasoning	Bennett, G. K. Seashore, H. G. Wesman, A. G.	Psychological Corporation
Employee Aptitude Survey Test #7—Verbal Reasoning (EAS #7)	Grimsley, G. Ruch, F. L. Warren, N. D. Ford, J. S.	Psychological Services, Inc.
The PSI Basic Skills Tests for Business, Industry, and Government: Decision Making (BST #6)	Ruch, W. W. Shub, A. N. Moinat, S. M. Dye, D. A.	Psychological Services, Inc.
The PSI Basic Skills Tests for Business, Industry, and Government: Reasoning (BST #10)	Ruch, W. W. Shub, A. N. Moinat, S. M. Dye, D. A.	Psychological Services, Inc.
Advanced Test Battery: Verbal Critical Reasoning (ATB-VA3)	Saville & Holdsworth, Ltd.	Saville & Holdsworth, Ltd.

12. Inductive Reasoning Tests

Test	*Author*	*Publisher*
Ball Aptitude Battery: Inductive Reasoning	Sung, Y. H. Dares, R. V.	The Ball Foundation
Figure Classification	not provided	Educational Testing Service
Letter Sets—I-1	not provided	Educational Testing Service
Location Test—I-2 Pattern Relations Test	not provided not provided	Educational Testing Service National Institute for Personnel Research
Advanced Test Battery: Numerical Critical Reasoning (ATB:NA4)	Saville & Holdsworth, Ltd.	Saville & Holdsworth, Ltd.
Critical Reasoning Test Battery (CRTB)	Saville & Holdsworth, Ltd.	Saville & Holdsworth, Ltd.

| MD5 Mental Ability Test: Alphabetical Sequence Relationships, Symbol Relationships (letters), Symbol Relationships (numbers), Relationships Between Numbers and Letters | Mackenzie Davey & Co. | The Test Agency |

13. Information Ordering Tests

Test	Author	Publisher
Calendar Test	not provided	Educational Testing Service
Following Directions	not provided	Educational Testing Service
Ordering I	cited in Guilford & Hoepfner (1971)	

14. Category Flexibility Tests

Test	Author	Publisher
New Uses (NU)	Hoepfner, R. Guilford, J. P.	Consulting Psychologists Press
Combining Objects—XU-1	not provided	Educational Testing Service
Different Uses—XU-4	not provided	Educational Testing Service
Making Groups—XU-3	not provided	Educational Testing Service
Substitute Uses—XU-2	not provided	Educational Testing Service
Halstead Category Test	Hill, M.	Precision People, Inc.

15. Speed of Closure Tests

Test	Author	Publisher
Concealed Words—CS-2	not provided	Educational Testing Service
Gestalt Completion Test—CS-1	not provided	Educational Testing Service

Comprehensive Ability Battery: Perceptual Completion	Hakstian, A. R. Cattell, R. B.	Institute for Personality & Ability Testing, Inc.
Closure Speed (Gestalt Completion)	Thurstone, L. L. Jeffrey, T. E.	London House Press
Graduate and Managerial Assessment: Abstract	The Hatfield Polytechnic	NFER-Nelson Publishing Co., Ltd.
Multidimensional Aptitude Battery: Picture Completion	Jackson, D. N.	Research Psychologists Press

16. Flexibility of Closure Tests

Test	Author	Publisher
Weber Advanced Spatial Perception Test (WASP)	Weber, P. G.	The Australian Council for Educational Research, Limited
Copying Test	not provided	Educational Testing Service
Hidden Figures Test—CF-1 (rev.)	not provided	Educational Testing Service
Hidden Patterns	not provided	Educational Testing Service
Comprehensive Ability Battery: Hidden Shapes	Hakstian, A. R. Cattell, R. B.	Institute for Personality & Ability Testing, Inc.
Closure Flexibility (Concealed Figures)	Thurstone, L. L. Jeffrey, T. E.	London House Press
Gottschaldt Figures Test	not provided	National Institute for Personnel Research
Work Aptitude: Profile and Practice Set: Using Your Eyes	Saville & Holdsworth, Ltd.	Saville & Holdsworth, Ltd.
Flanagan Aptitude Classification Tests (FACT): Components, Precision	Flanagan, J. C.	Science Research Associates
Flanagan Industrial Tests (FIT): Components	Flanagan, J. C.	Science Research Associates

17. Spatial Orientation Tests

Test	Author	Publisher
Guilford–Zimmerman Aptitude Survey: Spatial Orientation	Guilford, J. P. Zimmerman, W. S.	Consulting Psychologists Press
Right–Left Orientation	Benton, A. L.	Oxford University Press
Foster Mazes	not provided	Stoelting Co.
Project A (U.S. Army): Orientation Tests 1–3	cited in Olson (1990)	

18. Visualization Tests

Test	Author	Publisher
Minnesota Spatial Relations Test	American Guidance Service Test Division	American Guidance Service
Minnesota Spatial Relations Test (revised)	H. C. Link	American Guidance Services
Guilford–Zimmerman Aptitude Survey: Spatial Visualization	Guilford, J. P. Zimmerman, W. S.	Consulting Psychologists Press
Shapes Test	Morrisby, J. R.	Educational and Industrial Test Services, Ltd.
Card Rotations Test	not provided	Educational Testing Service
Cube Comparison Test	not provided	Educational Testing Service
Form Board Test—VZ-1	not provided	Educational Testing Service
Paper Folding—VZ-2	not provided	Educational Testing Service
Surface Development	not provided	Educational Testing Service
Complete Form Board Set	not provided	Lafayette Instrument Co., Inc.
O'Connor Wiggly Block	O'Connor, J.	Lafayette Instrument Co., Inc.

Judgment of Line Orientation	Benton, A.	Oxford University Press
Blox Test (Perceptual Battery)	not provided	National Institute for Personnel Research
Employee Aptitude Survey Test #5— Space Visualization (EAS #5)	Grimsley, G. Ruch, F. L. Warren, N. D. Ford, J. S.	Psychological Services, Inc.
Technical Test Battery: Spatial Reasoning (TTB: ST7)	Saville & Holdsworth, Ltd.	Saville & Holdsworth, Ltd.
Technical Test Battery: Spatial Recognition (TTB: ST9)	Saville & Holdsworth, Ltd.	Saville & Holdsworth, Ltd.
The Shapes Analysis Test	Heim, A. Watts, K. P. Simmonds, V.	The Test Agency Ltd.

19. Perceptual Speed Tests

Test	*Author*	*Publisher*
Guilford–Zimmerman Aptitude Survey: Perceptual Speed	Guilford, J. P. Zimmerman, W. S.	Consulting Psychologists Press
Finding A's Test—P-1	not provided	Educational Testing Service
Identical Pictures	not provided	Educational Testing Service
Number Comparison— P-2	not provided	Educational Testing Service
Job Effectiveness Prediction System: Coding and Converting (JEPS: Test Code K)	Personnel Decisions Research Institute for Life Office Management Association	Life Office Management Association

Job Effectiveness Prediction System: Comparing and Checking (JEPS: Test Code L)	Personnel Decisions Research Institute for Life Office Management Association	Life Office Management Association
Perceptual Speed (Identical Forms)	Thurstone, L. L. Jeffrey, T. E.	London House Press
Differential Aptitude Test: Perceptual Speed and Accuracy	Bennett, G. K. Seashore, H. G. Wesman, A. G.	The Psychological Corporation
Minnesota Clerical	Andrew, D. M. Patterson, D. G. Longstaff, H. P.	The Psychological Corporation
Employee Aptitude Survey Test #3—Visual Pursuit (EAS #3)	Grimsley, G. Ruch, F. L. Warren, N. D. Ford, J. S.	Psychological Services, Inc.
Employee Aptitude Survey Test #4— Visual Speed and Accuracy (EAS #4)	Grimsley, G. Ruch, F. L. Warren, N. D.	Psychological Services, Inc.
The PSI Basic Skills Tests for Business, Industry, and Government: Forms Checking (BST #9)	Ruch, W. W. Shub, A. N. Moinat, S. M. Dye, D. A.	Psychological Services, Inc.
The PSI Basic Skills Tests for Business, Industry, and Government: Visual Speed and Accuracy (BST #15)	Ruch, W. W. Shub, A. N. Moinat, S. M. Dye, D. A.	Psychological Services, Inc.

20. Selective Attention Tests

No standard tests of selective attention were identified.

21. Time Sharing Tests

No standard tests of time sharing were identified.

Psychomotor Abilities

22. Control Precision Tests

Test	Author	Publisher
Counter-Interval Timer (with Perceptualmotor Pen)	not provided	Lafayette Instrument Co., Inc.
Photoelectric Rotary Pursuit	not provided	Lafayette Instrument Co., Inc.
Purdue Hand Precision Test	not provided	Lafayette Instrument Co., Inc.
Rotary Pursuit Test	not provided	Lafayette Instrument Co., Inc.
Standard Rotary Pursuit	not provided	Lafayette Instrument Co., Inc.
Control Adjustment Test	cited in Fleishman (1964, 1972)	Prentice-Hall, Inc.

23. Multilimb Coordination Tests

Test	Author	Publisher
Two-Arm Coordination Test	not provided	Lafayette Instrument Co., Inc.
Control Adjustment Test	cited in Fleishman (1964, 1972)	Prentice-Hall, Inc.
Rudder Control Test	cited in Fleishman (1964, 1972)	Prentice-Hall, Inc.
Two-hand Coordination Test	cited in Fleishman (1964, 1972)	Prentice-Hall, Inc.

24. Response Orientation Tests

Test	Author	Publisher
Multi-Choice Reaction Time Apparatus	not provided	Lafayette Instrument Co., Inc.

Direction Control Test	cited in Fleishman (1964, 1972)	Prentice-Hall, Inc.
Discrimination Reaction Time Test	cited in Fleishman (1964, 1972)	Prentice-Hall, Inc.
Project A (U.S. Army): Reaction Time (Choice)	cited in Olson (1990)	

25. Rate Control Tests

Test	*Author*	*Publisher*
Comprehensive Ability Battery: Tracking	Hakstian, A. R. Cattell, R. B.	Institute for Personality & Ability Testing
Bassin Anticipation Timer	Bassin, S.	Lafayette Instrument Co., Inc.
Modified Bassin Timer	Bassin, S.	Lafayette Instrument Co., Inc.
Motor Judgment Test	cited in Fleishman (1964, 1972)	Prentice-Hall, Inc.
Single Dimension Pursuit Test	cited in Fleishman (1964, 1972)	Prentice-Hall, Inc.
Rate Control Test	cited in Fleishman (1964, 1972)	Prentice-Hall, Inc.

26. Reaction Time Tests

Test	*Author*	*Publisher*
Multi-Choice Reaction Time Apparatus	not provided	Lafayette Instrument Co., Inc.
Project A (U.S. Army): Reaction Time (Simple)	cited in Olson (1990)	

27. Arm-Hand Steadiness

Test	*Author*	*Publisher*
Steadiness Tester-Groove Type	not provided	Lafayette Instrument Co., Inc.

Steadiness Tester–Hole Type	not provided	Lafayette Instrument Co., Inc.
Track Tracing Test	cited in Fleishman (1964, 1972)	Prentice-Hall, Inc.
Flanagan Aptitude Classification Tests (FACT): Coordination	Flanagan, J. C.	Science Research Associates
Flanagan Industrial Tests (FIT): Coordination	Flanagan, J. C.	Science Research Associates

28. Manual Dexterity

Test	Author	Publisher
Minnesota Rate of Manipulation Tests	Employment Stabilization Research Institute, University of Minnesota	American Guidance Service
Manual Dexterity Test	E.I.T.S.	Educational and Industrial Test Services Ltd.
Card Sorting Box	not provided	Lafayette Instrument Co., Inc.
Hand Tool Test	not provided	Lafayette Instrument Co., Inc.
Minnesota Manual Dexterity Test	not provided	Lafayette Instrument Co., Inc.
Pennsylvania Bi-Manual	Roberts, J. R.	Lafayette Instrument Co., Inc.
Triangular Blocks	not provided	Lafayette Instrument Co., Inc.
Two-Arm Coordination Test	not provided	Lafayette Instrument Co., Inc.
Occupational Aptitude Survey and Interest Schedule: Manual Dexterity	Parker, R. M.	Pro-Ed
Hand-Tool Dexterity Test	Bennett, G. K.	The Psychological Corporation

Stromberg Dexterity Test (STD)	Stromberg, E. L.	The Psychological Corporation
FIT: Precision	Flanagan, J. C.	Science Research Associates
General Aptitude Test Battery (GATB): Manual Dexterity	U.S. Employment Service	U.S. Department of Labor
VCWS8-Simulated Assembly	not available	Valpar International Corporation

29. Finger Dexterity

Test	*Author*	*Publisher*
Ball Aptitude Battery: Finger Dexterity	Sung, Y. H. Dares, R. V.	The Ball Foundation
Grooved Pegboard	not provided	Lafayette Instrument Co., Inc.
Purdue Pegboard Test	Purdue Research Foundation	Lafayette Instrument Co., Inc.
Roeder Manipulative Aptitude Test	Roeder	Lafayette Instrument Co., Inc.
Fine Finger Dexterity Work Task Unit	not provided	Mississippi State Research & Training Center/ University Rehabilitation National Industries for the
Crawford Small Parts Dexterity Test (CSPDT)	Crawford, J.	The Psychological Corporation
Employee Aptitude Survey Test #9—Manual Speed and Accuracy (EAS #9)	Grimsley, G. Ruch, F. L. Warren, N. D. Ford, J. S.	Psychological Services, Inc.
Flanagan Aptitude Classification Tests (FACT): Finger Dexterity	Flanagan, J. C.	Science Research Associates
O'Connor Finger Dexterity Test	O'Connor, J.	Stoelting Co.

| O'Connor Tweezer Dexterity Test | O'Connor, J. | Stoelting Co. |
| General Aptitude Test Battery (GATB): Finger Dexterity | U.S. Employment Service | U.S. Department of Labor |

30. Wrist-Finger Speed

Test	Author	Publisher
Adult/Adolescent Finger Tapper	not provided	Lafayette Instrument Co., Inc.
Tapping Board	not provided	Lafayette Instrument Co., Inc.

31. Speed of Limb Movement

Test	Author	Publisher
Lafayette Pegboard	not provided	Lafayette Instrument Co., Inc.
Toggle Switch Device	not provided	Lafayette Instrument Co., Inc.
Two Plate Tapping	cited in Fleishman (1964)	Prentice-Hall, Inc.

Physical Abilities

32. Static Strength

Test	Author	Publisher
Ball Aptitude Battery: Grip Test	Sung, Y. H. Dares, R. V.	The Ball Foundation
Hand Dynamometer (Dynamometer Grip Strength Test)	not provided	Lafayette Instrument Co., Inc.
Jackson Strength Evaluation System	not provided	Lafayette Instrument Co., Inc.
Jamar Digital Hand Dynamometer	not provided	Lafayette Instrument Co., Inc.

Jamar Hydraulic Hand Dynamometer	not provided	Lafayette Instrument Co., Inc.
Nicholas Manual Muscle Tester	not provided	Lafayette Instrument Co., Inc.
Smedley Hand Dynamometer	not provided	Stoelting Co.

33. Explosive Strength

Test	Author	Publisher
Vertisonic	not provided	Lafayette Instrument Co., Inc.
Broad Jump	cited in Fleishman (1964)	Prentice-Hall, Inc.
50-yard Dash	cited in Fleishman (1964)	Prentice-Hall, Inc.
Shuttle Run	cited in Fleishman (1964)	Prentice-Hall, Inc.
Softball Throw	cited in Fleishman (1964)	Prentice-Hall, Inc.

34. Dynamic Strength

Test	Author	Publisher
Bachman Ladder	not provided	Lafayette Instrument Co., Inc.
Bent-Arm Hang	cited in Fleishman (1964)	Prentice-Hall, Inc.
Pull-ups	cited in Fleishman (1964)	Prentice-Hall, Inc.
Push-ups	cited in Fleishman (1964)	Prentice-Hall, Inc.
VCWS 19—Dynamic Physical Capacities	not provided	Valpar International Corporation

35. Trunk Strength

Test	Author	Publisher
Leg Lifts	cited in Fleishman (1964)	Prentice-Hall, Inc.
Sit–ups	cited in Fleishman (1964)	Prentice-Hall, Inc.

36. Extent Flexibility

Test	Author	Publisher
Sit & Reach	not provided	Health Education Services: Novel Products, Inc.
Arthrodial Protractor	not provided	Lafayette Instrument Co., Inc.
Computerized Digital Goniometer	not provided	Lafayette Instrument Co., Inc.
Digital Goniometer	not provided	Lafayette Instrument Co., Inc.
Finger Goniometer	not provided	Lafayette Instrument Co., Inc.
Flexibility Tester	not provided	Lafayette Instrument Co., Inc.
Kinesthesiometer	not provided	Lafayette Instrument Co., Inc.
Leighton Flexometer	not provided	Lafayette Instrument Co., Inc.
Pluri-Dig	not provided	Lafayette Instrument Co., Inc.
Plurimeter – V	Rippstein, J.	Lafayette Instrument Co., Inc.
Professional Goniometer Set	not provided	Lafayette Instrument Co., Inc.
Extent Flexibility Test ("Twist & Touch")	cited in Fleishman (1964)	Prentice-Hall, Inc.

37. Dynamic Flexibility

Test	Author	Publisher
Stability Testing and Rehabilitation Station	not provided	Lafayette Instrument Co., Inc.
Dynamic Flexibility Test ("Bend, Twist, & Touch")	cited in Fleishman (1964)	Prentice-Hall, Inc.

38. Gross Body Coordination

Test	Author	Publisher
Cable Jump Test	cited in Fleishman (1964)	Prentice-Hall, Inc.

39. Gross Body Equilibrium

Test	Author	Publisher
Basic Balance Beam	not provided	Lafayette Instrument Co., Inc.
Infrared Stability Platform	not provided	Lafayette Instrument Co., Inc.
Stability Platform	not provided	Lafayette Instrument Co., Inc.

40. Stamina

Test	Author	Publisher
Fitness Equipment 5000 Treadmill Test	not provided	Lafayette Instrument Co., Inc.
One-mile Run	cited in Fleishman (1964)	Prentice-Hall, Inc.
Step Test	cited in Cotten (1971)	Prentice-Hall, Inc.
600-Yard Run-Walk Test	cited in Fleishman (1964)	Prentice-Hall, Inc.

Sensory/Perceptual Abilities

41. Near Vision

Test	Author	Publisher
Industrial Short Tests	not provided	Keystone View, Division of Mast Development Co.
Near Point Landolt Ring Acuity Test	not provided	Keystone View, Division of Mast Development Co.
Near Point Sloan Letter Acuity Test	not provided	Keystone View, Division of Mast Development Co.
Near Point Snellen Letter Acuity Test	not provided	Keystone View, Division of Mast Development Co.
Near Point "Tumbling E" Acuity Test	not provided	Keystone View, Division of Mast Development Co.
O.E.P. Test Set	not provided	Keystone View, Division of Mast Development Co.
OVS (Industrial Screening) Test Set	not provided	Keystone View, Division of Mast Development Co.
OVS Rapid Screening Test	not provided	Keystone View, Division of Mast Development Co.
Physicians' Visual Rating Tests	not provided	Keystone View, Division of Mast Development Co.
Pilot Vision Test Set	not provided	Keystone View, Division of Mast Development Co.
Professional Performance Test Set	not provided	Keystone View, Division of Mast Development Co.
Visual Skills Test Set	not provided	Keystone View, Division of Mast Development Co.
Visual Survey Telebinocular (Vision Screening Telebinocular)	not provided	Keystone View, Division of Mast Development Co.
VSII (Vision Screener)	not provided	Keystone View, Division of Mast Development Co.

Bassin Anticipation Timer	not provided	Lafayette Instrument Co., Inc.
Professional Vision Tester	not provided	Lafayette Instrument Co., Inc.
Programmed Slide Sets	not provided	Lafayette Instrument Co., Inc.
Contrast Plus System	not provided	Stereo Optical Co.
Digital Acuity Test	not provided	Stereo Optical Co.
Optec 1000 & 2000	not provided	Stereo Optical Co.
Visual Functioning Assessment Tool (VFAT)	Costello, K. Pinkney, P. Scheffero, W.	Stoelting Co.
Titmus II Vision Tester: Professional Model	not provided	Titmus Optical Co./ Stereo Optical Co.
Visual Skills Test	not provided	Titmus Optical, Inc./ Stereo Optical Co.

42. Far Vision

Test	*Author*	*Publisher*
Driver Vision Test Set	not provided	Keystone View, Division of Mast Development Co.
Far Point Landolt Ring Acuity Test	not provided	Keystone View, Division of Mast Development Co.
Far Point Sloan Letter Acuity Test	not provided	Keystone View, Division of Mast Development Co.
Far Point Snellen Letter Acuity Test	not provided	Keystone View, Division of Mast Development Co.
Far Point "Tumbling E" Acuity Test	not provided	Keystone View, Division of Mast Development Co.
Industrial Short Tests	not provided	Keystone View, Division of Mast Development Co.
O.E.P. Test Set	not provided	Keystone View, Division of Mast Development Co.

OVS (Industrial Screening) Test Set	not provided	Keystone View, Division of Mast Development Co.
OVS (Rapid Screening) Test Set	not provided	Keystone View, Division of Mast Development Co.
Professional Performance Test Set	not provided	Keystone View, Division of Mast Development Co.
Physicians' Visual Rating Tests	not provided	Keystone View, Division of Mast Development Co.
Universal Driver Test	not provided	Keystone View, Division of Mast Development Co.
Usable Vision Binocular DB-1D	not provided	Keystone View, Division of Mast Development Co.
VSII (Vision Screener)	not provided	Keystone View, Division of Mast Development Co.
Visual Skills Test Set #5100	not provided	Keystone View, Division of Mast Development Co.
Visual Survey Telebinocular (Vision Screening Telebinocular)	not provided	Keystone View, Division of Mast Development Co.
Professional Vision Tester	not provided	Lafayette Instrument Co., Inc.
Bassin Anticipation Timer	Bassin, S.	Lafayette Instrument Co., Inc.
Programmed Slide Sets	not provided	Lafayette Instrument Co., Inc.
Contrast Plus System	not provided	Stereo Optical Co.
Digital Acuity Test	not provided	Stereo Optical Co.
Optec 1000 2000	not provided	Stereo Optical Co.
Visual Functioning Assessment Tool (VFAT)	Costello, K. Pinkney, P. Scheffero, W.	Stoelting Co.
Titmus II Vision Tester: Professional Model	not provided	Titmus Optical, Inc./ Stereo Optical Co.
Visual Skills Test	not provided	Titmus Optical Inc./ Stereo Optical Co.

43. Visual Color Discrimination

Test	Author	Publisher
City University Color Vision Test	Fletcher, R.	Keeler Instruments, Inc.
Driver Vision Test Set	not provided	Keystone View, Division of Mast Development Co.
Industrial Short Tests	not provided	Keystone View, Division of Mast Development Co.
O.E.P. Test Set	not provided	Keystone View, Division of Mast Development Co.
OVS (Industrial Screening) Test Set	not provided	Keystone View, Division of Mast Development Co.
OVS (Rapid Screening) Test Set	not provided	Keystone View, Division of Mast Development Co.
Physicians' Visual Rating Tests	not provided	Keystone View, Division of Mast Development Co.
Pilot Vision Test Set	not provided	Keystone View, Division of Mast Development Co.
Universal Driver Test	not provided	Keystone View, Division of Mast Development Co.
VSII (Vision Screener)	not provided	Keystone View, Division of Mast Development Co.
Visual Skills Test Set #5100	not provided	Keystone View, Division of Mast Development Co.
Color Blindness Test	not provided	Lafayette Instrument Co., Inc.
Ishihara Test for Color Blindness	not provided	Lafayette Instrument Co., Inc.
Professional Vision Tester	not provided	Lafayette Instrument Co, Inc.
Pseudoisochromatic Plates	not provided	Lafayette Instrument Co., Inc.
Stand Perimeter, Schweigger Type	not provided	Lafayette Instrument Co., Inc.

Dvorine Color Vision Test	Dvorine, I.	The Psychological Corporation
Farnsworth Dichotomous Test for Color Blindness	Farnsworth, D.	The Psychological Corporation
AO Pseudo-Isochromatic Color Test	not provided	Richmond Products
Contrast Plus System	not provided	Stereo Optical Co.
Optec 1000 & 2000	not provided	Stereo Optical Co.
Titmus II Vision Tester: Professional Model	not provided	Titmus Optical Inc./ Stereo Optical Co.
Visual Skills Test	not provided	Titmus Optical Inc./ Stereo Optical Co.

44. Night Vision

Test	Author	Publisher
Multivision Contrast Tester (MCT)	Ginsburg, A.	Visitech Consultants, Inc./ Stereo Optical Co.

45. Peripheral Vision

Test	Author	Publisher
Field Analyzer	not provided	Allergan-Humphries
Periometer	not provided	Keystone View, Division of Mast Development Co.
VSII (Vision Screener)	not provided	Keystone View, Division of Mast Development Co.
Optec 1000	not provided	Stereo Optical Co.
Visual Functioning Assessment Tool (VFAT)	Costello, K. Pinkney, P. Scheffero, W.	Stoelting Co.
Wayne Saccadic Fixator	not provided	Wayne Engineering

46. Depth Perception

Test	Author	Publisher
Driver Vision Test Set	not provided	Keystone View, Division of Mast Development Co.
Industrial Short Tests	not provided	Keystone View, Division of Mast Development Co.
O.E.P. Test Set	not provided	Keystone View, Division of Mast Development Co.
OVS Rapid Screening Test	not provided	Keystone View, Division of Mast Development Co.
Physician's Visual Rating Tests	not provided	Keystone View, Division of Mast Development Co.
Professional Performance Test Set	not provided	Keystone View, Division of Mast Development Co.
Stereopsis—DB-6D	not provided	Keystone View, Division of Mast Development Co.
Universal Driver Test	not provided	Keystone View, Division of Mast Development Co.
VSII (Vision Screener)	not provided	Keystone View, Division of Mast Development Co.
Visual Skills Test Set #5100	not provided	Keystone View, Division of Mast Development Co.
Depth Perception Apparatus	not provided	Lafayette Instrument Co., Inc.
Professional Vision Tester	not provided	Lafayette Instrument Co., Inc.
Contrast Plus System	not provided	Stereo Optical Co.
Optec 2000	not provided	Stereo Optical Co.
Stereofly Test	not provided	Stereo Optical Co.
Visual Functioning Assessment Tool (VFAT)	Costello, K. Pinkney, P. Scheffero, W.	Stoelting Co.

Randot Stereopsis Test	not provided	Titmus Optical, Inc./ Stereo Optical Co.
Stereo Fly Stereopsis Test	not provided	Titmus Optical, Inc./ Stereo Optical Co.
Visual Skills Test	not provided	Titmus Optical, Inc./ Stereo Optical Co.

47. Glare Sensitivity

Test	Author	Publisher
Multivision Contrast Tester (MCT) 8000	Ginsburg, A.	Visitech Consultants, Inc./ Stereo Optical Co.

48. Hearing Sensitivity

Test	Author	Publisher
Audiometer	not provided	Lafayette Instrument Co., Inc.
Seashore Measures of Musical Talents	Seashore, C. E.	The Psychological Corporation

49. Auditory Attention

Test	Author	Publisher
Goldman–Fristoe–Woodcock Auditory Skills Test Battery	Goldman Fristoe Woodcock	American Guidance Service
Technical Tests of Central Auditory Abilities	Flowers, A.	Perceptual Learning Systems
Code Distraction Task	cited in Fleishman & Friedman (1957a, 1957b)	

50. Sound Localization

No standard tests of sound localization were identified.

51. Speech Recognition

Test	Author	Publisher
Lindamood Auditory Conceptualization Test (LAC)	Lindamood & Lindamood	DLM Teaching Resources
Wichita Auditory Fusion Test (WAFT)	McCroskey, R.	Modern Education Corporation
Tree/Bee Test of Auditory Discrimination (Tree/Bee Test)	Fudala, J. B.	United Educational Services, Inc.

52. Speech Clarity

Test	Author	Publisher
Oral Speech Mechanism Screening Examination (OSME)	St. Louis, K. Ruscello, D. M.	Pro-Ed
Test of Minimal Articulation Competence (T-MAC)	Secord, W.	The Psychological Corporation

Section III

Publishers' Addresses

Allergan-Humphries
3081 Teagarden Street, San Leandro, CA 94577
(415) 895-9110

American Guidance Services
4201 Woodland Road, P.O. Box 99, Circle Pines, MN 55014
(612) 786-4343, (800) 328-2560

The Australian Council for Educational Research Limited
Radford House, Frederick Street, Hawthorn, Victoria 3122, Australia
(03) 819 1400

The Ball Foundation
Building C-120, 800 Roosevelt Road, Glen Ellyn, IL 60137
(708) 469-6270

Consulting Psychologists Press, Inc.
3803 East Bayshore Road, P.O. Box 10096, Palo Alto, CA 94303
(800) 624-1765, (415) 969-8901

Critical Thinking Press and Software (formerly Midwest Publications, Inc.)
P.O. Box 448, Pacific Grove, CA 93950
(408) 375-2455

CTB/McGraw Hill
Publishers Test Service, Del Monte Research Park, 2500 Garden Road,
Monterey, CA 93940
(408) 649-8400 (in CA), (800) 682-9222 (in CA), (800) 538-9547

DLM Teaching Resources
P.O. Box 4000, One DLM Park, Allen, TX 75002
(800) 442- 4711 (in TX), (800) 527-4747

Educational and Industrial Test Services, Ltd.
83 High Street, Hemel Hempstead, Herts, HP1 3AH, England
(0042) 56773

Educational Evaluation Enterprises
Awre, Newnham, Gloucestershire GL14 1ET, England
(0594) 510503

E.F. Wonderlic Personnel Test, Inc.
820 Frontage Road, Northfield, IL 60093
(708) 446-8900

Educational Testing Service
Rosedale Road, Princeton, NJ 08541
(609) 921-9000

Human Resource Research Organization (HumRRO)
1100 South Washington Street, Alexandria, VA 22314
(703) 549-3611

Industrial Psychology, Inc.
515 Madison Avenue, New York, NY 10022
(212) 355-5330

Institute for Personality and Ability Testing
1801 Woodfield Drive, Savoy, IL 61874
(217) 352-4739

Keeler Instruments, Inc.
456 Parkway, Lawrence Park Industrial District, Broomall, PA 19008
(800) 523-5620

ystone View, Division of Mast Development Co.
?212 East 12th Street, Davenport, IA 52803
¹9) 326-0141

'nstrument Co., Inc.
· 5729, Lafayette, IN 47903
'505

ement Association (LOMA)
v Road, Atlanta, GA 30327

line, IL 61244

Lafayette Instrument Co., Inc.
P.O. Box 5729, Lafayette, IN 47903
(317) 423-1505

Life Office Management Association (LOMA)
5770 Powers Ferry Road, Atlanta, GA 30327
(404) 951-1770

LinguiSystems, Inc.
3100 4th Avenue East, Moline, IL 61244
(800) ALL-TIME

London House Press
1550 North Northwest Highway, Park Ridge, IL 60068
(800) 323-5923

McCartney, William A.
P.O. Box 507, Kaneohe, HI 96744
(808) 239-8071

Mississippi State University Rehabilitation Research & Training Center
P.O. Drawer 6189, Mississippi State, MS 39762
(601) 325-2001

Modern Education Corporation
P.O. Box 721, Tulsa, OK 74101
(918) 584-7278

National Institute for Personnel Research
P.O. Box 32410, Braamfontein, 2017 Republic of South Africa
(011) 339-4451

NFER-Nelson Publishing Co., Ltd.
Darville House, 2 Oxford Road East, Windsor, Berkshire SL4 1DF, England
(07535) 58961

Oxford University Press
200 Madison Avenue, New York, NY 10016
(212) 679-7300

Perceptual Learning Systems
P.O. Box 864, Dearborn, MI 48121
(212) 277-6480

Precision People, Inc.
3452 North Ride Circle South, Jacksonville, FL 32217
(904) 262-1096

Prentice-Hall
Rt. 9-W Englewood Cliffs, NJ 07632
(201) 592-2000

PRO-ED
8700 Shoal Creek Boulevard, Austin, TX 78758
(512) 892-3142

The Psychological Corporation
    Order Service Center, P.O. Box 839954, San Antonio, TX 78283
    (800) 228-0752

Psychological Services, Inc.
    370 Lake Forest Road, Bay Village, OH 44140
    (216) 871-7663

Research Psychologists Press, Inc.
    1110 Military Street, P.O. Box 610984, Port Huron, MI 48061-0984
    (800) 265-1285

Richardson, Bellows, Henry, & Co., Inc.
    1140 Connecticut Avenue N.W., Suite 610, Washington, D.C. 20036
    (202) 659-3755

Richmond Products
    1021 South Rodgers Circle, Suite #6, Boca Raton, FL 33487-2894
    (407) 994-2112

The Riverside Publishing Co.
    8420 Bryn Mawr Avenue, Chicago, IL 60631
    (800) 323-9540

Saville & Holdsworth Ltd.
    3 AC Court, High Street, Thames Ditton, Surrey, KT70SR, England

Science Research Associates
    155 North Wacker Drive, Chicago, IL 60606
    (312) 984-7000

Sheridan Psychological Services, Inc.
    P.O. Box 6101, Orange, CA 92667
    (714) 639-2595

SPECTRA Communication Associates
    P.O. Box 5031, Contract Station 20, New Orleans, LA 70018
    (504) 831-4440

Stoelting Co.
    620 Wheat Lane, Wood Dale, IL 60191
    (708) 860-9700

Stereo Optical Co.
3539 North Kenton Avenue Chicago, IL 60641-3879
(800) 344-9500

The Test Agency
Cournswood House, North Dean, High Wycombe, Bucks, HP14 4NW,
England
(024) 3384

Titmus Optical Co.
P.O. Box 191, Petersburg, VA 23803
(800) 446-1802

U.S. Army Research Institute (ARI)
5001 Eisenhower Avenue, Alexandria, VA 22333

U.S. Department of Defense
Testing Directorate, Headquarters, Military Entrance Processing Command,
Attn: MEPCT, 2500 Green Bay Road, North Chicago, IL 60064
(800) 323-0513

U.S. Department of Labor
Division of Employment and Training Administration, 200 Constitution Ave.,
Washington, D.C. 20210
(202) 523-6871

United Educational Services, Inc.
P.O. Box 357, East Aurora, New York 14052
(800) 458-7900

Vistech Consultants, Inc.
4162 Little York Road, Dayton, OH 45414-2566
(800) 847-8324

Valpar International Corporation
P.O. Box 5767, Tucson, AZ 85703
(800) 528-7070

Wayne Engineering
1825 Willow Road, Northfield, IL 60093-2925
(708) 441-6940

Section IV

References

Aiken, L. R. (1988). *Psychological testing and assessment.* Boston: Allyn & Bacon, Inc.

Anastasi, A. (1988). *Psychological testing* (6th ed.). New York: Macmillan.

Carroll, J. B. (1980). *Individual difference relations in psychometric and experimental cognitive tasks* (Report No. 163). Chapel Hill, NC: The L. L. Thurstone Psychometric Laboratory, University of North Carolina.

Conoley, J. C. & Kramer, J. J. (Eds.). (1989). *The tenth mental measurement yearbook.* Lincoln, NE: Buros Institute of Mental Measurements of the University of Nebraska-Lincoln.

Cotten, D. J. (1971). A modified step test for cardiovascular testing. *Research Quarterly, 42,* 91–95.

Cronbach, L. J. (1990). *Essentials of psychological testing.* New York: Harper & Row.

Ekstrom, R. B., French, J. W., & Harman, H. H., with Dermen, D. (1976). *Manual for kit of factor-referenced cognitive tests.* Princeton, NJ: Educational Testing Service.

Ekstrom, R. B., French, J. W., & Harman, H. H. (1979). Cognitive factors: Their identification and replication. *Multivariate Behavioral Research Monographs, No. 79–2.*

Fleishman, E. A. (1964). *The structure and measurement of physical fitness.* Englewood Cliffs, NJ: Prentice Hall.

Fleishman, E. A. (1975). Toward a taxonomy of human performance. *American Psychologist, 30*(12), 1127–1149.

Fleishman, E. A. (1972). Structure and measurement of psychometric abilities. In R. N. Singer (Ed.), *The psychomotor domain: Movement behavior.* Philadelphia, PA: Lee & Febiger.

Fleishman, E. A. (1982). Systems for describing human tasks. *American Psychologist, 37*(7), 821–834.

Fleishman, E. A. (1988). Some new frontiers in personnel selection research. *Personnel Psychology, 41*(4).

Fleishman, E. A. (1992). *The Fleishman-Job Analysis Survey (F-JAS).* Palo Alto, CA: Consulting Psychologists Press.

Fleishman, E. A., and Friedman, M. P. (1957a). *Some standardized tests of auditory perceptual abilities* (Research Report No. AFPTRC-TN-57-132). Lackland Air Force Base, TX: Air Force Personnel and Training Research Center.

Fleishman, E. A., and Friedman, M. P. (1957b). *The development of the Air Force aural code test* (Research Report No. AFPTRC-TN-57-133). Lackland Air Force Base, TX: Air Force Personnel and Training Research Center.

Fleishman, E. A., & Mumford, M. D. (1988). Ability requirements scales. In S. Gael (Ed.), *The job analysis handbook for business, government, and industry.* New York: Wiley.

Fleishman, E. A., & Mumford, M. D. (1989). Abilities as causes of individual differences in skill acquisition. *Human Performance, 2*(3), 201–222.

Fleishman, E. A., & Mumford, M. D. (1991). Evaluating classifications of job behavior: A construct validation of the ability requirements scales. *Personnel Psychology, 44,* 523–575.

Fleishman, E. A., & Quaintance, M. K. (1984). *Taxonomies of human performance: The description of human tasks.* Orlando, FL: Academic Press, Inc.

Fleishman, E. A., & Reilly (1992). *Administrator's guide for the Fleishman Job Analysis Survey* (F-JAS). Palo Alto: Consulting Psychologists Press.

Guilford, J. P., & Hoepfner, R. (1971). *The analysis of intelligence.* New York: McGraw-Hill.

Harman, H. H. (1975). *Final report of research on assessing human abilities* (Report No. PR-75-20). Princeton, NJ: Educational Testing Service.

Katz, J. (Ed.) (1985). *Handbook of clinical audiology* (3rd ed.). Baltimore, MD: Williams & Wilkins.

Linn, R. E. (Ed.) (1989). *Educational measurement* (3rd ed.). New York: Macmillan.

Mitchell, J. V., Jr. (1983). *Tests in print III: An index to tests, test reviews, and the literature on specific tests.* Lincoln, NE: Buros Institute of Mental Measurements, University of Nebraska-Lincoln.

Olson, D. M. (1990). *Project A: A summary* (ARI Publication No. 9227). Alexandria, VA: U.S. Army Research Institute.

Psychological tests and special education materials (1989). Stoelting Co., Wood Dale, IL.

Schemmer, F. M. (1982). *Development of rating scales for selected vision, auditory, and speech abilities* (Report No. ARRO-3064-FR). Bethesda, MD: Advanced Research Resources Organization.

Sternberg, R. J., & Smith, E. E. (1988). *The psychology of human thought.* Cambridge, MA: Cambridge University Press.

Stephens, S. D. G. & Prasansuk, S. (1988). Measurement in hearing and balance: Vol. 5. In Hoke, M. (Ed.), *Advances in audiology.* Basel, Switzerland: Karger.

Stubblefield, J. (1987). *"Hear": Hearing evaluation and referral: A manual for helping the "non-audiologist" perform valid and accurate hearing tests.* Tulsa, OK: Modern Education Corporation.

Sweetland, R. C. & Keyser, D. J. (Eds.) (1986). *Tests: A comprehensive reference for assessment in psychology, education, and business* (2nd ed.). Kansas City, MO: Test Corporation of America.

Weldon, L. J., Yarkin-Levin, K., & Fleishman, E. A. (1982). *Abilities and tests potentially related to the maintenance of electronic equipment* (Report No. 3081). Bethesda, MD: Advanced Research Resources Organization.

Yost, W. A., & Nielsen, D. W. (1985). *Fundamentals of hearing* (2nd ed.). New York: Holt, Rinehart & Winston.

Section V

Indexes of Tasks and Jobs
Cited in the Text

Tasks Index

Jobs Index

Errata
This replaces pages 131 and 132.

About the Authors

Edwin A. Fleishman (Ph.D., The Ohio State University) is internationally known for his research on human abilities and the analysis of work requirements. He is currently Distinguished University Professor of psychology at George Mason University. Earlier he was President of the Advanced Research Resources Organization and prior to this was Director of The American Institutes for Research in Washington, DC. Formerly, Dr. Fleishman was a professor at Yale University, and has been a visiting professor at the University of California, Irvine, and the Israel Institute of Technology.

Dr. Fleishman is the author of more than two hundred journal articles, monographs, and research reports, including the books *Studies in Personnel and Industrial Psychology*, *Psychology and Human Performance* (with R. M. Gagné), *The Structure and Measurement of Physical Fitness*, *Current Developments in the Study of Leadership* (with J. G. Hunt), and *Taxonomies of Human Performance* (with M. Quaintance). He has been editor-in-chief of the *Journal of Applied Psychology* and has served on the editorial boards of the journals *Personnel Psychology*, *Organizational Behavior and Human Performance*, *Computers in Human Behavior*, *Human Performance*, and *Leadership Quarterly*.

Dr. Fleishman has been elected president of three Divisions of the American Psychological Association, including the Division of Industrial and Organizational Psychology (SIOP), the Division of Evaluation and Measurement, and the Division of Engineering Psychology, and for eight years he was the president of the International Association of Applied Psychology. He has also served as Chair of APA's Committee on Psychological Tests and Assessment. He has been a consultant to numerous industrial, educational, and government organizations, has served on the Advisory Panel on Psychology and the Social Sciences in the Office of the Secretary of Defense, and serves on the Board of Examiners of the U.S. State Department.

In 1980, Dr. Fleishman was the recipient of the American Psychological Association's Distinguished Scientific Award for the Applications of

Psychology. In 1982, the University of Edinburgh awarded him the Honorary Doctor of Science Degree. In 1984, he received the annual Distinguished Professional Contributions Award from the Society of Industrial and Organizational Psychology. In 1986, he was a Visiting Senior Scholar under an award from the Japanese Society for the Promotion of Science.

Maureen E. Reilly (M.A., George Mason University) is currently working as a research assistant in the Center for Behavioral and Cognitive Studies at George Mason University while she is completing work for her Ph.D. in industrial/organizational psychology. She is also a consortium research fellow working at the Army Research Institute, where she is carrying out research on personnel selection, performance assessment, and turnover reduction.